SHIP

NEW-YORK
JAN
21

Due 3 cents.
Due 6 cents.

JUIN

PD 16

CARRIE
SEP
28
8TH.

Smithsonian Institution Press, Washington, D.C.

American Issue

The U.S. Postage Stamp, 1842–1869

Peter T. Rohrbach and Lowell S. Newman

Library of Congress Cataloguing in Publication Data

Rohrbach, Peter T.
   American issue.

   Bibliography: p.
   Includes index.
   1. Postage-stamps—United States—History—19th century. 2. Postal service—United States—History—19th century. I. Newman, Lowell S. II. Title.
HE6185.U5R63
1984   769.56973   83–27146
ISBN 0–87474–816–X

Printed in the United States of America

Designed by Carol Hare Beehler

The paper in this book meets the guidelines for permanence and durability of the Committee on Production Guidelines for Book Longevity of the Council on Library Resources.

Contents

Introduction

IN EARLY-NINETEENTH-CENTURY AMERICA, THE POSTAL SERVICE HAD become a vital part of the nation's life, providing the common thread which bound the young republic together.

During those days, before the instant electronic communications systems we now take for granted, the mail was the principal means by which business and personal and political communications could be delivered over the ever-widening distances of a rapidly developing country. At first by foot, and then by postrider, and finally by wagons and stagecoaches, the growing postal system kept pace with the settlers as the frontier moved westward. Next, the iron horse of the railroads replaced its flesh and blood counterpart as the prime carrier of the mails, and steamboats also plied the coastal and inland waterways with loads of mail for post offices along their routes.

In the early 1840s, major postal reforms were instituted in England which resulted in cheaper rates and wider use of the mails in that country. These same types of reforms were gradually introduced into the United States during the 1840s and 1850s, and as postal rates dropped and the areas of service were expanded, more and more Americans began to use the mails.

One of the principal features of the British reforms was the introduction of the world's first adhesive postage stamp, and soon this innovation was introduced in the United States as America began to produce its own first adhesive postage stamps. The present book is a chronicle, told in text and illustrations, of those early American postage stamps, beginning with the first stamps in 1842 and ending with the issue of the first American pictorial stamps in 1869. However, this is more than just a story of the physical stamps themselves: it is a story of the stamps in their own time, showing how they were an integral part of the great postage reforms and advances of the era.

The quarter of a century chronicled in this book certainly covers some of the most troubled years in the nation's history, but the positive advances made in postal communications during that era have had profound and lasting effects on the very life of the nation. Even now, over one hundred years later, the changes which occurred during those years from 1842 to 1869 form the basis of our modern postal system. The extent to which modern society has come to depend upon postal systems was probably best stated by Herbert Samuel, a former postmaster general of Great Britain, in his introduction to A.D. Smith's classic work, *The Development of Rates of Postage*:

> *The whole of our social organization has come to depend in large degree upon the post. Commerce, in all its departments, relies upon it. All the variety of associations which are, in their wide expansion, distinctive of modern civilization and necessary to its life and energy—employer's associations, trade unions, co-operative societies, friendly societies, religious bodies, political and propagandist organizations of every kind, local, national, and international—the whole nervous system of the modern state, depends upon the quick transmission of information and ideas: it would never have reached and could not maintain its present development without cheap, reliable, and speedy means of communication.*

Seen in this light, the development of the American postal system is a fascinating reflection of the growth and development of our nation from its days as an infant republic, through the course of a bitter civil war, until it finally emerged as a modern state.

The postage stamp played a pivotal role in that process, and it will be the main focus of this book. First, however, we will review briefly the early American postal system and the British reforms of the 1840s, and then we will see how postal reform was developed in the unique American postal system of this new nation with its own special demands of a growing population and expanding frontiers. And, as our chronicle continues, we will also study the key and interesting figures of the reform, the people who molded the American post and its stamps into the effective and "democratic" system it remains to this day.

Most of all, we will discuss those early American postage stamps themselves, which have become the most familiar embodiment of postal service for millions of Americans. Tracing it from its British origins, we will see the postal adhesive take root in America, first as a private and local issue in 1842, and later under the auspices of the federal government, and we will follow it through its many issues and improvements over its first quarter of a century. The Civil War saw the issuance of stamps by both sides in the conflict, but after the war there was yet another development in the American stamp: the pictorial stamp. Now, instead of confining itself to portraits of great American leaders, the United States stamp also offered pictorial designs. Those early pictorials presented historical and patriotic themes which, in a special way, reasserted the unity of the recently divided nation. By that time, however, the American postal system had reached the end of its first major era, and was then a vital part of a growing republic.

This is the story of that era—a time when the first American postage stamps were being issued.

I The American Postal System, 1639 to 1840— An Overview

IN THE TWO CENTURIES IN AMERICA BEFORE THE FIRST STAMPS WERE issued, the postal service performed a necessary and indispensable role in the birth and development of the new nation.

At first, during the earliest days of postal service in colonial North America, there was only a fragmentary system within the Massachusetts Bay Colony. In 1639 the General Court of the Colony had ordered that all mail to and from England was to be left at Richard Fairbank's Tavern in Boston. This embryonic mail system, actually nothing more than a centralized location for distribution of letters, was of service only to the immediate area. The last half of the seventeenth century saw the development of a few postal routes connecting major population centers throughout the colonies. Early routes were operated by local authorities until a central postal organization was established for all of the colonies in 1691.

In 1753 Benjamin Franklin, previously the postmaster at Philadelphia, was appointed by the Crown as joint postmaster general for the North American Colonies, along with William Hunter. Franklin was to serve as postmaster general for twenty-one years, until 1774 when he was dismissed because of actions sympathetic to the cause of the rebellious colonists. The service provided by the posts in these early years was rarely reliable and the postage rates were so high that few of those colonists who could write were able to afford the luxury of regular correspondence.

The Second Continental Congress appointed Franklin postmaster general of its own postal system in 1775. After only one year Franklin was succeeded by his son-in-law, Richard Bache, who was in turn shortly followed by Ebenezer Hazard, the last postmaster general prior to the end of the Confederation period. The disruptions of the Revolution and the attendant deterioration of the economy placed a great strain upon the postal services of this period. Rates of postage increased to ridiculous levels as the currencies of the various colonies fell in value, and even those few that could afford the rates put their trust in God first, rather than the post office, for the safe delivery of their letters.

〰〰

With the ratification of the Constitution in 1789, Samuel Osgood of Massachusetts became the first postmaster general of the United States of America. At that time there were only seventy-five post offices and fewer than 2,000 miles of post roads in the entire nation. During the next fifty years the General Post Office, as the department was then known, experienced rapid expansion both in terms of the area serviced and the volume of mail carried. The young republic was growing fast, and as settlements spread beyond the eastern coastal region, the post routes went along, providing the settlers with their only links to the centers of population and government in the East. Rates during the early days of the constitutional post had stabilized at a high, but not prohibitive, level.

In 1815 the postage rates were raised 50 percent in order to replenish the treasury, which had been depleted by the War of 1812. This war tax was eliminated after one year, and rates were soon reduced even further as the postal system reached a level of use that allowed for cost-effective operation of routes in the densely populated East. The fact that profitable routes in the East were in effect subsidizing the less heavily used postal routes to the western settlements was a major complaint among eastern businessmen. Congress consistently ignored their pleas for more reasonable rates on profitable lines, because the revenue from those lines was needed to make the postal system as a whole break even. This policy had two effects on the nation and its postal system. First, it encouraged the settlement of the West by providing an affordable means of communication with the East. Second, the great disparity between the cost of mail transport in the East, and the rates charged for service over those routes, encouraged the formation of numerous private mail delivery companies which operated in direct competition with the government posts for many years.

〜〜〜

When Amos Kendall of Kentucky was appointed postmaster general in 1835 he was faced with growing public dissatisfaction with the nation's postal system. One of the prime areas of concern was the postal rate structure, which was considered to be too complex and the rates too high, especially in relation to the national economy, then in the midst of a severe recession.

Postal charges were based on mileage and the number of sheets per letter, rather than on weight. For distances over 400 miles, for instance, the charge was twenty-five cents. That rate doubled for two sheets, and tripled for three sheets, and so on.

Furthermore, the mail was usually sent unpaid, and the recipient would only pay the postage when it arrived. There were exceptions, especially in the case of an important business letter or in the case of a love letter, when the postage was prepaid, but more often the recipient paid the charge when he went to the post office to inquire if he had any mail. A congressional act of 1794 had provided for the local delivery of mail for an additional payment of two cents per letter, but apparently few postmasters, apart from those in some large cities, availed themselves of local delivery. The post office was the place to mail and pick up letters.

In the face of what they considered excessive postal rates, many people tried to circumvent the charge. Sometimes, friends or acquaintances would carry their mail by hand on the stagecoaches for them, or sometimes the stagecoach drivers themselves would hand-carry mail. Other abuses derived from the fact that the recipient did not have to accept the mail at the post office; he could, after inspecting it unopened, simply reject it. This added to the growing pile of unclaimed mail around the country.

There were a number of artifices which could be employed. For instance, a stagecoach traveler might tell his family that he would send a letter on arrival, letting them know of his safe journey, and the family would later refuse the traveler's subsequent letter at the post office, knowing that the intended message had been sent and received. Also, a system of codes was often worked out on the face of the envelope which gave the information the sender wanted to impart. Sometimes the code—a dot or a line, perhaps—gave the simple *yes* or *no* answer the sender wished to convey; other codes might indicate that the letter inside was important and should be paid for and opened. Another code was the use of a misspelled word. As a result of these subterfuges, a large amount of mail went unclaimed after being inspected by the intended recipient, and the post office had to incur the cost of transporting the mail without any reimbursement.

In the years prior to Amos Kendall's term as postmaster general, another practice was achieving great popularity: the use of postmarking handstamps. The earliest postmasters had marked the folded letters—or "covers," as they are called in philatelic terms—with pen and ink to indicate either *paid* or *due*, but in the eighteenth century, handstamps were introduced which allowed the postmaster to print those notations on the envelope, along with the name of the post office. These handstamped impressions on the envelope were called "stamps," although they were not, of course, the adhesive postal stamps which were to come in use later. As early as 1792, Postmaster General Timothy Pickering remarked: "with respect to stamps for the post office, they are so useful, I wish every office would use them."

These postmarking devices became even more prevalent in the nineteenth century; in addition to saving the time required to write town names and dates at busy post offices, the handstampers produced more legible postmarks. At first, these handstamped markings tended to be in the straight-line style, but by Kendall's time it was more usual to find the mark done in the circular style. There was a great variety of styles in these postal markings, and attractive oval or pictorial markings were used by some postmasters. There were also some handstamps devised to indicate the actual rate to be charged in order to eliminate the task of writing the rates by hand, but they were used by only a few post offices because the complex rate structure, whereby the mileage and number of sheets had to be computed, required too many different handstamps to be convenient.

Only three examples of this straight-line handstamped marking from George Town (on the shore), Maryland, have been reported. The "S" at the end of the name is meant to differentiate the small Eastern Shore village from the busy port on the Potomac River which bore the same name. The postage due when the letter was delivered at the Philadelphia post office was six pence sterling, equal to two pennyweights of coined silver, the rate for single letters traveling between sixty and one hundred miles. As was the case with most covers of this early period, the town marking on the April 11, 1776 cover was applied to the back, while the notation of the postage due was marked on the front of the wrapper. (National Philatelic Collection)

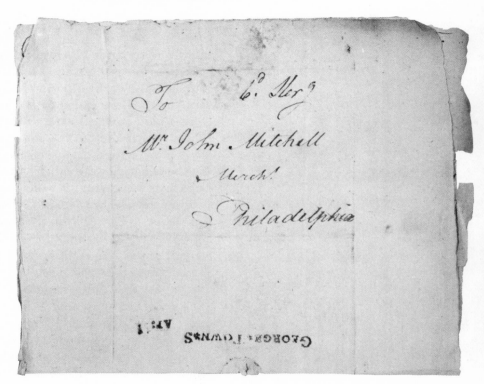

This fancy boxed marking from Little River Lick, Arkansas Territory, is only known to have been used in 1832. Prestamp period markings showing the month, day, and year are quite uncommon. On this cover the March 3, 1832, date is composed of mixed upper- and lower-case letters, and the first "3" is inserted upside down and backward. The twenty-five-cent postage for a single letter sent more than 400 miles was prepaid. (National Philatelic Collection)

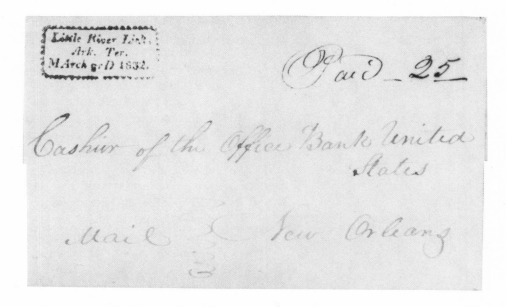

But Kendall was to find that handstamps, no matter how attractive they were or how they expedited the mails, were not a solution to the nagging problems of the mail service. Kendall, at age fifty-one, was a powerful figure in Washington who was not at all averse to confronting a difficult problem. He had been born in Massachusetts, but after graduation from Dartmouth College and an apprenticeship at law, he followed the westward flood of migration from New England, ending up in Kentucky. He first practiced law, but in 1816 he became editor of the *Argus of Western America* in Frankfort, a newspaper which was to attain great influence throughout the state under his direction. In the presidential election of 1828, the paper endorsed Andrew Jackson, and when Jackson carried Kentucky that year he attributed his victory there in no small part to Kendall's support.

As a reward, Kendall was selected to carry Kentucky's electoral vote for Jackson to Washington in 1828, and as was the case with so many other political figures over the years, he would remain there for the rest of his life. During the first six years of the Jackson administration, Kendall served as an auditor at the Treasury. He acquired a reputation as an extremely capable administrator, and he was able to institute reforms at the Treasury after uncovering corruption on the part of his predecessor. This accomplishment allowed, at least in appearance, the Jackson administration to make good on its campaign promises. But Kendall had an even more important role to play behind the scenes in Washington, where he belonged to a group of Jackson's closest advisors popularly known at the time as the "Kitchen Cabinet." He was also the President's unofficial speech writer, and the Jackson papers in the Library of Congress clearly show that Kendall had a large share in the preparation of at least five of the annual messages.

In 1835, during Jackson's second term when his popularity was becoming seriously damaged by reports of corruption among some of his appointees, the President had another task for Amos Kendall to perform: his appointment as postmaster general came at a time when there were growing complaints about the postal service. It was a challenge Kendall accepted with his usual enthusiasm.

Taking on the postmaster general's job in a reformer's mood, Kendall intended to use his powerful position in Washington to accomplish his goals. (Since Jackson's first year in office in 1829, postmasters general had been members of the cabinet.) Unlike his very earliest precedessors, who had wanted to operate the Post Office Department as a high-profit-making arm of the government, Kendall tended to agree with most of the later postmasters general who, although they certainly would like to have seen a profit, placed delivery of the mails as the highest priority. As a matter of fact, during most of Kendall's five-year term, the Post Office Department showed a deficit and had to be subsidized by the Treasury.

One of his first tasks was a reorganization and restructuring of the Post Office Department itself, and the new organizational structure Kendall devised was to remain in operation for many years without significant changes. He also cleaned up the bookkeeping in the department, and paid off many delinquent debts.

Kendall found not only that the nation was growing in size, but also that a new transportation mode was at hand: the sound of the railroad train whistle was being heard in the land. In 1828 the Baltimore & Ohio became the first American passenger railroad, and soon the mail was being carried on the rails. Kendall decided to use this new means of transportation, and in 1835 the Post Office awarded its first mail contract to the railroads. As more miles of tracks were laid each year, more mail would be carried by rail, rather than by stagecoach, post rider, or steamboat. The changeover was gradual, however, and up to the time of the Civil War there would still be more miles of stagecoach mail routes in the East than rail miles, but the

final outcome was obvious to Kendall: railroads would be the main carriers of the mail in the future.

In 1838 he lobbied Congress until it declared that year that all rail-

*The express mail services of 1836–39 are sometimes called the "Eastern Pony Express." For triple the regular postage rates, letters were transported by the fastest possible means to their destinations. This service was most commonly used for long distances and, after October 31, 1837, all letters sent by express had to be prepaid. The notation "Express" or "Express Mail" was generally written on the face of the cover, but this example from Milledgeville, Georgia, bears a strike of the scarce handstamped "*EXPRESS*" marking. The rate on this letter, bearing military orders to General Charles Floyd, was $1.12½, a double-letter rate for transit of between 150 and 400 miles. Rates ending in odd ¼¢, ½¢, and ¾¢ amounts were necessitated by the scarcity of United States coinage, and the exchange rates for Spanish and British coins, which were then in wide use. (National Philatelic Collection)*

roads were to be "post roads," and it specifically authorized mail contracts with railroad companies. The previous year he had placed route agents on the railroads to service the pouched mail between cities and to receive letters directly from patrons en route.

He also established a special service for areas where railroad and stagecoach service did not link up continuously or swiftly enough. This express service of 1836–39 has been called the "Eastern Pony Express" by historians in order to distinguish it from the more romantic "Western" Pony Express of some twenty-four years later, and it used riders on horseback and round-the-clock schedules between the major cities of the East and St. Louis, New Orleans, Mobile, and Charleston. These were special services, not intended to supplant the regular routes, and they were used chiefly by businessmen who wanted fast news of commodity price fluctuations, especially in the cotton market. For this service, the charge was three times the normal rate of postage.

Despite all his accomplishments, there was one case in which Kendall was severely criticized by Abolitionists in the North. It was discovered that postmasters in the South were removing from the mail and throwing away anything they considered to be antislavery propaganda, whether newspapers, pamphlets, or letters. This was clearly illegal, of course, and it was brought to Kendall's attention. However, Kendall, the New Englander become southerner, refused to take any action against the southern postmasters all the time he was in office.

And there was still that vexatious problem Kendall had not been able to solve—the large number of letters still being carried "out of the mails," to use the term of the day. The term denotes that large amount of mail which was not carried by the Post Office Department, but rather by individual travelers, stagecoach drivers, postriders, and now even by railroad employees. And, of course, there was also that unacceptably large amount of unclaimed mail, much of it part of the system to avoid postal charges by using coded envelopes. Kendall regarded all of this as illegal and as severely detrimental to the efficient postal system the young Republic needed.

Early in 1840 Kendall was intrigued by reports emanating from England: there was news of an English postal reform act which contained, among other things, required prepayment of postage along with the introduction of special stationery and adhesive stamps to indicate that the postage had been paid. These radical changes of postal policy in England sparked Amos Kendall's interest because of their possible application to the United States postal system, which he knew was badly in need of reform.

In order to get more information on the British reforms, Kendall decided to send a representative to England. The man chosen for this mission was George Plitt, a career postal employee who over the years was used for many special projects, notably the investigation of major cases of mail robbery and postal fraud. The Plitt report on the postal reforms in Great Britain was to be the first major step on the long road toward the eventual reform of the American postal rate structure and the issuance of the first American postage stamps.

II *The Plitt Report of 1840*

WHAT GEORGE PLITT, THE GOVERNMENT CAREERIST, DISCOVERED when he reached England in 1840 was that postal reform there was more than merely a rate-structure change in a governmental department; it was part of the great social-reform movement being carried out in England during the first half of the nineteenth century.

The author of the postal reform was Rowland Hill, a forty-four-year-old schoolmaster and educator, who was an outspoken proponent of the Radical movement in England. He seemed to have backed into postal reform from the rear door while he was considering possible tax-reform measures. He and his brothers, one of them a member of Parliament, had embarked on a study of the British tax-revenue system, and they found that in 1835 there had been a large surplus of revenue. Starting from that point, Hill began to review the various sources of tax revenues to see which could be reduced in order to alleviate the individual tax burden of the people. His study finally brought him to the postal system, and to his surprise he found there more than he had bargained for.

The postal rates in England, like those in America, were based on mileage, but, unlike the later postal authorities in America, the English government viewed postal charges as an important source of tax income for the government. Accordingly, the rates were extremely high, which discouraged the average citizen from using the postal system. Hill was able to chart the usage of the system throughout the century, and he found that its growth did not at all keep up with the growing economy and population. His first findings, therefore, were that the English postal system was overpriced and underused.

He also discovered the same abuses that existed in the American system: the subterfuges to avoid payment, such as coded covers and unclaimed mail, and the letters carried "out of the mails." There was also a particular abuse in that more class-conscious society: many people of importance and privilege had the right to send their mail free, and these "franks" were widely and illegally used for sending letters of people who did not have the franking privilege.

Apart from the tax restructuring with which he started, Hill now found that postal reform was a cause to burn in the heart of a Radical reformer. Not only should it afford tax relief, but it should also make the mails more readily available to the common man, and not be the property of the privileged few. Hill then embarked on an extensive research into all aspects of the postal system, and in January of 1837 he published a pamphlet calling for truly radical reforms, *Post-Office Reform: Its Importance and Practicality.*

The pamphlet was originally issued privately for circulation in the political and official circles to which Hill had ready access. Through the influence of his brother Matthew, the M.P., he was invited to give evidence before the Commissioners for Post Office Inquiry, but his reform proposals were not viewed favorably by the government, and they were resolutely opposed by the postmaster general and high officials at the Post Office. Then, as a true reform Radical, Hill decided to take his case directly to the people, and he issued the pamphlet publicly. It met with immediate, widespread, and influential support, and was enthusiastically supported by the press, the chambers of commerce, and other important bodies. Public meetings were

BRADSHAW'S
MANCHESTER JOURNAL.

Number 15.]   SATURDAY, 7TH AUGUST, 1841.   [Price 1½d.

PORTRAITS OF PUBLIC CHARACTERS.—No. VI.

ROWLAND HILL, ESQ.

held throughout England which resulted in numerous petitions to Parliament. Finally, in November 1837, the government was forced to appoint a Select Committee of the House of Commons to examine the reform proposals of Rowland Hill.

The fundamental features of the reforms contained in the Hill pamphlet were a fixed rate not based on mileage and a prepaid postage fee. Hill introduced statistics to indicate that the average cost of distributing a letter in Great Britain at that time was one and one-half pence, and that included the costs for large numbers of newspapers and franked letters, which were carried free. He called it "the natural cost of conveying a letter," and demonstrated by statistics that the actual cost of carrying a letter from London to Edinburgh was no more than one-thirty-sixth of a pence, rather than the rate of one shilling-one pence, which was then being charged.

Hill then proposed a uniform rate of one pence based on the weight of the letter, rather than on the number of sheets or the distance it was carried. He dismissed distances as a minor factor in costs, saying that actual costs really depended on the number of letters carried. Furthermore, postal employees spent a great deal of time-consuming and costly effort calculating mileage from one city to another, writing the charge on the letter, and attempting to collect the fee. Those costs could be saved, he said, if it was realized that more revenues would accrue because of the increased use of the lower-costing mails; thus the government would not suffer any serious tax liability.

In arguing for a prepaid fee, Hill again cited the time-consuming work of postal employees in collecting fees, but he also noted the many abuses of the present system whereby people were able to avoid postal fees. To remedy this, he suggested that the government sell envelopes and special stationery which had been imprinted with a government revenue stamp indicating that the postage had been paid. Then, almost as an afterthought, he added that anyone who did not have an envelope, or who wished to use his own stationery, could be sold "a bit of paper just large enough to bear the stamp and covered at the back with a glutinous wash, which the bringer might, by applying a little moisture, attach to the back of the letter." Thus, with this "bit of paper," came the initial suggestion for the postal adhesive.

As one might suspect, the merchants of stationery were loud in their complaints against a system that could easily put many of their number out of business. To smooth the ruffled feathers of the stationers, it was agreed that the use of the prepaid wrappers would not be as highly stressed in the actual use of the new system. Another objection, somewhat humorous in retrospect, was voiced by the editors of *Chamer's Edinburgh Journal*:

> *The author [referring to Hill's pamphlet] proceeds to show that a large share of the expenses of management is incurred in the business of collection, and that, to get quit of this, all letters must be paid on being put into the post office. . . . We consider this as perhaps one of the most visionary schemes ever put forth by a writer on finance. Mr. Hill, like most political economists, commits the blunder of making no allowance for the passions, the feelings, the habits, the prejudices and stupidities of mankind. At present, everybody knows how to put a letter into the post-office; but under the system proposed, only a section of the people would know how to proceed. Reader, imagine for a moment the idea of everyone*

having to buy stamped covers beforehand for his letters, or having to pay a penny with every letter he submitted to the inspection of an officer-keeper! You here see that nothing like delicacy of feeling, or the preservation of secrecy, is taken into account; every soul who sends a letter by post comes under the scrutiny of an officer of government.

But that is not all; the payment of the penny is fully as solid an objection. People will pay postage when they get a letter, their feelings at the moment inducing them to give any reasonable sum that is demanded, but few like to pay money along with a letter. As small as a penny is we believe that it would be grudged severely by many, and its exaction would in effect ruin the whole project. We are sorry for this, because it would be a fine simple cheap plan to make everyone post-pay his letters; but looking at human society as at present constituted, we are assured it would never work.

The Select Committee of the House of Commons issued its report in August 1838, recommending the adoption of Hill's proposals, but the national economy was not as healthy as in previous years and the government took no action. Hill, however, rallied the members of the Radical party in Parliament and they gained the votes needed for passage in exchange for their continued support of the government. The postal reform act embracing Hill's proposals was passed in 1839 and it became effective on January 10, 1840. The new rates were: one penny for letters of up to one-half ounce in weight; two pence for up to one ounce; and two pence for each additional ounce or fraction thereafter.

The prestamped stationery authorized by the act was issued in early May of 1840. The envelopes and wrappers had been designed by William

This small cover, franked with a penny black used on October 27, 1840, carried a letter from Charles Dickens, the famous author, to publisher Edward Moxon. The letter contained an order for books which Dickens wished to add to his personal library. (Richard B. Krakaur collection)

Mulready, a well-known painter and member of the Royal Academy, but the elaborate line drawing depicting the various benefits of the postal reform was widely criticized by the public. Stationers were quick to issue their own unstamped satirical parodies of the government's design, and the Mulready design was soon replaced with a dignified portrait of Queen Victoria within an oval frame.

For the optional "bits of paper," a design showing a profile portrait of the twenty-one-year old Victoria was chosen. Based upon the William Wyon medal of 1837 and engraved by Charles and Fredrick Heath (from a drawing by Henry Corbould), the stamps were printed by the firm of Perkins, Bacon, and Petch. The one-penny stamps were printed in black on white paper and quickly earned the nickname of "penny black," which they carry to this day.

For the two-pence stamps, a rich blue ink was used with the same design (except for the value tablet). Difficulties soon arose with the penny blacks because the cancellations applied at the post office were so hard to see against the black design that many people began to reuse the canceled stamps. The color was then changed to a reddish brown, solving the problem of reuse of stamps, at least for a short time.

To Hill's surprise, and no doubt to the delight of stationers everywhere, the "bits of paper" proved to be much more popular than the postal stationery. Although there were earlier uses of postal stationery of which Hill and his contemporaries were unaware (for example, Paris in 1653 and Sardinia in 1818), the use of adhesive labels in earlier periods had only extended to

The first postage stamps, along with the Mulready envelopes and letter sheets, were scheduled for release on May 6, 1840. Shipments of the new items were sent to British post offices well in advance of the release date, and some postmasters sold and accepted the stamps and stationery earlier. This one-penny Mulready was mailed prior to the official first day, forwarded from Wilton-Mowbry, and was received at Leicester on May 4, 1840, two days before the official release date. (National Philatelic Collection)

the realms of tax collection and parcel delivery (England in the late seventeenth century). The penny black and two-pence blue are thus rightfully regarded as the world's first adhesive postage stamps.

The British postal reforms, particularly the lower rates and the adhesive stamps, were so popular that letter mail doubled in the first year of their use.

The elaborate design of the new postal stationery was widely criticized in the press, and stationers were quick to issue their own satirical designs in imitation of the official issue. This example of a "Madeley" caricature envelope poked fun at the British involvement in the opium trade. The design of this envelope, first produced in June 1840, was similar enough to the official issue in terms of layout that it went through the mails without postage being collected. (National Philatelic Collection)

George Plitt returned to Washington with the Hill pamphlet and his own glowing report, which urged the United States to adopt the new British rate system and create an American postal adhesive. Amos Kendall read the report and agreed with Plitt's conclusions, but he knew that it would take a great deal of time and a major lobbying effort to convince Congress that the reforms should be adopted. Time was the crucial factor, something Kendall could not afford to squander, because in 1840 there were other problems requiring his immediate attention. Postal reform and the issuance of postage stamps would have to wait for a few more years.

III The Adhesive Comes to America, 1842

AMOS KENDALL WAS MORE THAN THE HEAD OF A GOVERNMENT DEpartment in Washington: he was, as we have noted, very much the political animal, supporting Jackson actively for the presidency in 1828 and working for his reelection in 1832. In 1836, when President Jackson had to step down because the custom of a two-term limitation in office was in force, Kendall supported another winning Democrat, Martin Van Buren. In 1840, however, the political picture did not appear as serene as it had four years earlier when Van Buren was first elected, defeating William Henry Harrison, a Whig, by almost one hundred electoral votes. Running for reelection, Van Buren again faced William Henry Harrison. The new race seemed to be very close, and Kendall had real fears that after twelve years the Democrats were on the verge of being turned out of the White House.

For the past year, Kendall had, in addition to his duties as postmaster general, taken over as editor of the *Extra Globe*, the Democratic newspaper in the nation's capital. But now, with the election upcoming, he decided he had to give full time to the newspaper and Van Buren's campaign. He could always return to government after Van Buren was reelected. Kendall thus resigned as postmaster general, and in his place Van Buren appointed John M. Niles, a sixty-three-year-old former United States senator from Connecticut. Later, Amos Kendall's worst fears were indeed realized when Van Buren lost the election, winning only sixty electoral votes to Harrison's 234. Kendall himself would never return to government service.

After the Democrats' defeat in 1840, John Niles was a lame-duck postmaster general, and although he was much impressed by the Plitt report, which he found on his desk when he took over, he was not to have any success in implementing it during his few months in office. In early 1841 he began to lobby Congress for postal reforms and the issuance of the first United States postage stamp, but the nation was still reeling from the severe depression of the late 1830s and Congress was in no mood to consider proposals which might well reduce tax revenues. A report from the period says that his proposals were greeted with "ridicule." The first U.S. stamps would still have to wait.

In 1841 the incoming President, William Henry Harrison, appointed as his postmaster general Francis Granger, a forty-nine-year-old Whig congressman from Connecticut. The new postmaster bore an illustrious name in postal affairs: his father was Gideon Granger, who had himself been postmaster general for thirteen years in the administrations of Jefferson and Madison. The senior Granger, serving as postmaster general from 1801 to 1814, had held that office longer than any other person in the history of the young nation, and he had proved himself to be a capable and successful administrator.

However, the young Granger was not to have much opportunity to see if he could emulate his father's record, because of Harrison's incredibly short term as President. The sixty-eight-year-old new President caught pneumonia during his inauguration ceremonies of March 4, 1841, and he died a month later. John Tyler, the Vice-President and a Whig from Virginia, succeeded him, but he quickly alienated the Whig leadership, notably by his veto of a bank bill. In protest, all the members of his cabinet resigned on

September 11, with the exception of Secretary of State Daniel Webster, and Tyler was forced to seek new cabinet members, including yet another postmaster general.

Tyler finally nominated Charles Wickliffe, a fifty-three-year-old former governor and congressman from Kentucky, who was to remain postmaster general for the remaining years of Tyler's single term in office. In 1841 Wickliffe studied the Plitt report with its enthusiastic recommendations of postal reform and postage stamps, but he wanted more information than was contained in the original report; he wanted some hard statistics on what the reform had really meant financially to the British government now that it had been in effect for over a year. What he learned about the British experience since the inception of the reform was not reassuring to him.

Despite the fact that the number of letters mailed in England had doubled in the first year, the financial loss to the Treasury was greater than Rowland Hill had predicted in the first year. The number of letters mailed increased from 82 million pieces to 169 million, but the Treasury had a reduction in net revenue of one million pounds sterling. In 1839, tax revenues from the mail had been £1,500,000, while under the new system in 1840 they dropped to £500,000. Although this had been about three times the size of the initial tax loss Hill had predicted, he was not particularly disturbed by these figures. He was now viewing postal reform primarily as a major social reform which would allow greater numbers of people to use the mail, and he was confident that tax revenues would increase as still more people began to use the new postage stamps.

Back in Washington, however, Charles Wickliffe did not regard these figures quite as benignly as Rowland Hill. Reviewing the U.S. postal figures during Amos Kendall's term, Wickliffe discovered that since 1837 the department had showed a deficit, and if he were to adopt a plan like Hill's in England, with its postage stamps and fixed lower rate providing revenues a third of those in previous years, he might well *triple* the amount of postal deficit in America. And tripling the amount of the deficit that the preceding administration had generated was something Charles Wickliffe could not abide for his department. He rejected the Plitt report as unsuitable for America.

It has been suggested that Wickliffe's rejection of the Plitt report was politically motivated, that he discarded it merely because it was a plan devised under the auspices of a previous and opposing political administration, but that seems too severe an interpretation to put upon it. More accurately, it appears that Wickliffe was quite sincere in his opposition to the Plitt report. He had started out as a Kentucky lawyer, known for his decisive thinking and the outspoken profession of his views, and he had also acquired a reputation as a haughty and rather disdainful individual. During his years in Washington he carried the nickname of "the Duke." He was also a committed Whig, and the Whigs favored fiscal conservatism and high tariff rates. The Duke was not about to reduce tariffs, which could very well cause a substantial loss of tax revenues; thus, federal postage reform would have to wait for yet another administration and another postmaster general.

But the inaction during Wickliffe's tenure did not mean that the issue was dead in America; on the contrary, there was considerable public agitation for postal reform. An association was formed in New York to work for the adoption of reduced postage rates, and meetings were held in large cities on the eastern seaboard. One of the continuing complaints of the cosmopolitan easterners was that their high postal costs were still subsidizing the mail on the western frontiers.

Even Rowland Hill, writing from England, became involved in the American postal cause, and he kept up a correspondence with reform leaders. Hill expressed the view that the American postmasters general, unlike their counterparts in England, had for some time not regarded postal charges as a major source of tax revenue, and therefore America should be even more ripe for postal reform than England had been. He did, however, recognize the fact that there were differences in the two countries, including the enormously greater distances traversed by mail routes in the new country, and he suggested that perhaps his "penny post" of England might be too low a tariff in America. The English pence was then the equivalent of two cents in America, but instead of proposing a two-cent postage rate, the reformers usually suggested a basic rate of five cents.

Meanwhile in England, during the years of Wickliffe's tenure, the use of the mails and postal revenue had continued to increase rapidly, as Rowland Hill had indeed predicted. By 1844, at the end of Wickliffe's term, the number of letters sent annually in England had tripled over the number sent in the last prereform year of 1839; and that figure would quadruple by 1847, with some 322 million letters being sent annually.

What the United States government was reluctant to do was finally accomplished in 1842 by private enterprise: *the first issuance of an American adhesive postal stamp.*

The origin of this first American adhesive stamp is part of another phenomenon of early 1840s, the rapid growth of the private mail companies—sometimes offering local delivery in a particular city and sometimes offering intercity delivery—which were usually able to deliver mail in less time and for less cost than the U.S. mail. Initially, Charles Wickliffe in Washington did not seem to be particularly bothered by these private posts, which continued to proliferate during his four-year term.

One of the more successful of these private postal companies was founded in Boston, principally by William F. Harnden, who in 1839 inaugurated a Boston-New York mail service. But by 1844 there were more than forty of these companies operating in the Boston area alone. One of the largest firms was Hale & Company, which provided service from New England to Washington, D.C., and branch service to Buffalo. Letters were usually picked up by company carriers and delivered to the door at the point of destination, even if that was in a distant city—and all for cheaper and quicker delivery than that offered by the United States post. Often these private companies used the handstamps described in the last chapter to mark the mail they carried.

One of the smaller intracity private posts of the era was the *New York Penny Post*, which operated in New York City in 1840–41. A local-delivery post, it used a handstamp of a double-lined circle, which was inscribed with, "NEW YORK" at the top, "PENNY POST" at the bottom, and the day, month, and posting time in the center. This New York firm was to have an important role in the development of the first United States adhesive stamp, because a certain visiting Englishman had his eye on it.

The Englishman was Henry Thomas Windsor, a British merchant who had sailed from Liverpool in April 1841, reaching New York in May of that year. He planned to stay in the United States for a year or two, traveling to see some of its more interesting places, and making his headquarters in Hoboken, New Jersey. One of the things that struck Henry Windsor about America was its inferior postal system, especially when compared to the reforms that he had seen recently in England. There were no postage stamps here, and the official rates were too high.

He confided his impressions to a friend, New York stockbroker Alexander M. Greig, and explained the system of Rowland Hill, which was then being used in England. It could work here—and Windsor, the English merchant, saw a wonderful business opportunity for using Hill's system in America with a local private post company. Alexander Greig was impressed with Windsor's description of the Hill plan, and he was fascinated with the idea of creating a U.S. postage stamp. The economics of it made sense, too, because Greig realized that the high U.S. postal rates were partly caused by the extremely high costs of transporting small amounts of mail over the great distances on the frontiers. But those costs would not exist in high-volume mail in a single city like New York, and thus extremely competitive postal charges could be offered.

The two men agreed to a partnership to see if they could introduce the Hill plan to America. Windsor offered to undertake the actual management

Thomas O'Connor Esqr

34 St Mark's Place

When the Post Office Department bought Greig's City Despatch Post in mid-1842, it also acquired the New York delivery company's supply of the first adhesive stamps used in America. After resuming operations as the United States City Despatch Post on August 17, the company used the same stamps, which thus became the first official United States stamps. This cover bears a copy of the three-cent City Despatch Post stamp canceled with the new-style "U.S. CITY DESPATCH POST" handstamp at one o'clock on August 25, 1842, the ninth day of government operation. (R. Meyersburg collection)

of the project; what he wanted mostly from Greig was his name. He said that the project would have a greater chance of success if the postal service was introduced under the name of a well-known New Yorker, rather than a visiting Londoner. Greig readily agreed to the proposal, and was more than happy to leave the management of the firm to Windsor, because the Englishman had actually seen the plan in operation in Great Britain and Greig himself had no experience at all in postal matters. Thus, although Greig was listed as the founder of their company, and the resultant postal service was often referred to as "Greig's Post," the original concept and the actual management of the post was the work of Henry Windsor.

The first thing to be done was to acquire an existing private postal service, which would eliminate the time-consuming problem of establishing a delivery service from the ground up. The two men decided on the New York Post, and in late 1841 they acquired the firm, naming it the City Despatch Post, with headquarters at 46 William Street in New York City. The plan was to open for business on February 1, 1842, in order to be in operation before St. Valentine's Day, when they could expect a great volume of mail. In preparing for their first deliveries they placed boxes for the deposit of letters in public places throughout the city, and they inserted advertisements in the newspapers. The rate for the delivery of mail within New York City was established at three cents, and following the Hill plan, prepayment would be offered. That also implied the creation of a postage stamp.

The 1842 City Despatch Postal Stamp was engraved and printed in sheets of forty stamps each, without perforations, in grayish black ink on grayish to white paper. Some of those sheets had adhesive on the back, while others

Charles Wickliffe, postmaster general, 1841–1845.

probably did not. The stamps were sold for three cents each, or $2.50 per hundred—and that, of course, constituted prepayment for letters dropped in the boxes around the city, a new feature which became quite popular. The stamp design displayed a portrait of George Washington contained in a double-lined oval frame. Above the portrait was the inscription "CITY DESPATCH POST," and below the portrait were the words "THREE CENTS." Both inscriptions were in serifed capital letters, and between the upper and lower inscriptions at each side was an ornament. This three-cent design was the only one issued by the City Despatch Post.

The new service proved an instant success, and the post was immediately swamped with Valentine mail, so much so that an advertisement under Greig's name was placed in the newspapers, apologizing for any inconveniences caused by the "enormous influx of letters" received on St. Valentine's day "notwithstanding ten additional carriers were on duty." Following the initial success of the large St. Valentine's Day mailing, the firm continued to gain even more users, and an advertisement in the *New York Herald* for March 31 indicates the kind of service the City Despatch Post was offering to its customers:

Principal Office.—
Letters deposited before half past 8, half past 12, and half past 3 o'clock will be sent out for delivery at 9, 1 and 4 o'clock.

Branch Offices.—
Letters deposited before 7, 11 and 2 o'clock will be sent out for delivery at 9, 1 and 4 o'clock.

Alex M. Greig, Agent

By the summer of that year of 1842, the City Despatch Post, with its new, easy-to-use postage stamps, had taken over a substantial share of the local postal market in New York City. In July the firm was handling about 450 letters a day, while the government carriers at the New York Post Office were handling only 250 per day.

The first American adhesive postal stamp had now been successfully launched, and it is ironic that in America it was not done by a social reformer, as in England with Rowland Hill, nor was it even done by a government interested in providing a faster and less expensive means of communications for its citizens, but rather by an intinerant British merchant and a local stockbroker who saw the opportunity to do something profitable which should have been done a long time ago.

There was one other thing the City Despatch Post accomplished: it finally caught the attention of Charles Wickliffe in Washington, and the Duke expressed some real concern that this upstart new service was, after six months, carrying almost twice as much mail in New York as his own post office. *At last*, it was time for him to take some action. However, that action did not include anything as incisive as the issuance of government postage stamps or the reduction of government postal rates in order to become competitive with the City Despatch Post. Rather, reverting to tactics he had employed while a young lawyer in Bardstown, Kentucky, where he had acquired a reputation for hard-fisted dealing, Wickliffe contacted the postmaster of New York, John Lorimer Graham, and gave him specific orders regarding what to do about the City Despatch Post—*buy them out*.

Accordingly, Graham approached Alexander Greig, the proprietor of record, and began negotiations for the government to purchase the City Despatch Post and all its assets. It has been suggested that the government exerted some undue pressure on the New York stockbroker and his English partner to sell out after only a few months, but there is no evidence of that; rather, it seems that the two partners viewed it as a means of making a quick and profitable return on their investment. Furthermore, Henry Windsor had been in America over a year now, and his original intention had been to remain in the country for no more than two years. Taking a profit and returning home apparently appealed to him.

John Graham told Greig that he would like to take over his firm and then unite it with the United States Post Office, continuing to issue under federal auspices the same kind of postage stamp Greig and Windsor had created earlier that year. He offered Greig $1,200 for the City Despatch Post and all its assets. To sweeten the deal, he also offered Greig a post office position as supervisor of the new combined Despatch-government operation. The salary offered was $1,000 a year, but apparently realizing that Greig did not have much experience in postal matters, nor did he intend to acquire any, Graham made the added offer that Greig would hold this new position jointly with William Seymore, who was a seasoned post office official. The offer was attractive to Greig: he would get the quick return on his investment; he would receive a new title and a new salary; and he would be supported in that position by someone who really knew how to do the job. He accepted.

On July 21 Graham wrote to Wickliffe in Washington, telling him of

The first stamps printed with the authorization of the United States government were the U.S. City Despatch Post three-cent blacks on "rosy buff" paper. This stamp, with a light strike of the boxed U.S. handstamp over the central portrait, is the only known used copy. The rare "rosy buff" paper variety has often been considered to be a trial color of the new stamps, but this used copy proves that at least one of the stamps produced on this paper saw actual use. (R. Meyersburg collection)

Greig's acceptance and asking for written authorization to spend the $1,200 for the purchase of the City Despatch Post out of the general receipts of the New York Post Office. He also noted that the price agreed upon "was considerably under cost," which it undoubtedly was. Graham went on to tell Wickliffe that he thought the new combined venture could be quite profitable for the department because if he could add the Despatch's more than 450 daily letters to his own mail, he felt he should be able to make a profit of about $2,400 a year after expenses on this service. He also said that he thought the new name for this venture should be the *United States City Despatch Post*. Finally, he suggested an easy means for the conversion: "By doing this, all the boxes, stamps, etc., already in possession of Mr. Greig can be used, by simply adding the words "United States" to the stamps and labels on the boxes."

Wickliffe readily agreed to all the terms, and on August 13 Alexander Greig placed an ad in the New York newspapers announcing the sale of his service to the federal government. He assured his readers that "the accommodation and convenience of the public will be effectively maintained" in the new postal service. He said that the service he started would now be performed by the United States Government, and in the name of "the proprietors," he thanked his clients for "the very generous and efficient support." Finally, he added, "All stamps issued by the City Despatch Post will be received by the Government."

The United States City Despatch Post officially began operations on August 16, 1842, and by November of that year it was delivering 762 letters a day. It serviced an area of the city measuring about three square miles,

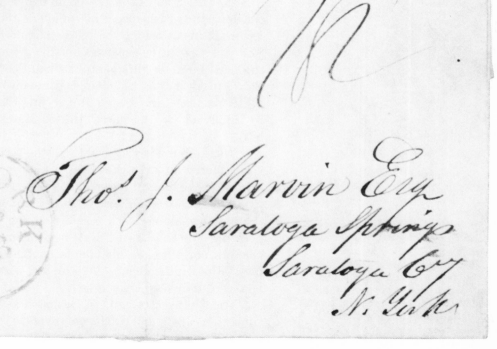

On this cover, the three-cent U.S. City Despatch Post stamp, printed in black on greenish blue paper, paid for carrier service "to the mails." Once the cover reached the New York post office, it entered the mail system as an unpaid letter, the postage of 18¾¢ to be collected from the addressee in Saratoga Springs, New York. (R. Meyersburg collection)

and within that area were 112 stations with collection boxes which were emptied three times a day. There were also three deliveries a day.

Stamps were sold at the same price as the original City Despatch Post, three cents each, and at the outset Graham's suggestion was followed in which the old Despatch stamps were used, sometimes with the addition of the words "United States." However, when that supply was exhausted, the United States City Despatch Post printed its own stamps, and continued to do so throughout the four years of its existence. These stamps were basically the same as the original Despatch stamps, with a portrait of George Washington displayed in a double-lined oval frame, the inscription "UNITED STATES CITY DESPATCH POST" on the top of the oval, and "THREE CENTS" at the bottom. These stamps were printed in black on rosy-buff, blue, and green colored paper, and also on blue, dark blue, green, and apple-green glazed-surface colored paper.

During those four years, therefore, the federal government was in the curious position of operating a postal service in New York that issued adhesive postage stamps, which were popularly received and financially successful, while at the same time the federal postal system itself did not issue any stamps. Throughout his tenure in office, Wickliffe made no move toward issuing federal postage stamps, even though they were then flourishing in England and starting to be imitated by other countries, such as Brazil, which issued its first stamps in 1843. However, the Duke had accomplished one thing by his purchase of the New York Despatch City Post: he had bought out the opposition. And the opposition here was the first American adhesive postal stamp.

The history of the New York Despatch Post from that point on was brief.

On November 28, 1846, an announcement appeared in New York City newspapers: "By the authority of the Postmaster General the United States City Despatch Post is discontinued." The federal government was terminating its operation and selling the business back to the private sector. By that time, Wickliffe was long gone from the federal government, and conditions had changed significantly. For one thing, there had been a proliferation of private postal companies in New York. For another, there was a new mood in the Post Office Department in Washington: the postal reform act of 1845 had been passed, and the department was in the process of preparing to issue the first federal adhesives the following year. The United States City Despatch Post had become a period piece.

The United States City Despatch Post in New York City was bought by Abraham B. Mead, a former government letter carrier, who renamed it the Post Office City Despatch, and it began operations on November 30, 1846. Operating out of an office located at the corner of Liberty and Nassau streets opposite the U.S. Post Office, Mead offered the same basic type of service the Despatch had been providing for years, including pickup boxes throughout the city and thrice-daily collections and delivery.

The postage stamps issued by Mead were printed from the original City Despatch Post plates of 1842 with the word "THREE" altered to "TWO." The stamps of the Post Office City Despatch were issued in two colors—black on green-glazed surface paper; and black on pink-glazed surface paper.

The following year, Mead sold his firm to Charles Coles, who again changed the name, reverting to the original name of 1842, the City Despatch Post. Offering the same general type of service, he operated out of an office at 492 Broadway, near the corner of Broome Street.

For his stamps, Coles used the original 1842 Despatch plate as altered by Mead in 1846, but he had the plate further altered by the addition of his initial "C," on each side of the portrait of Washington. The initials were punched into the plate and they sometimes appeared inverted or sideways. Coles's stamps were printed in a variety of colors—green, grayish white, vermilion, yellow, and buff. These City Despatch Post stamps first appeared in late 1847 or early 1848.

Cole's City Despatch Post—the descendant of the firm which issued the first American adhesive postal stamp—was not destined to have a long history, and it gradually faded from the scene. It is difficult to find any trace of it after 1851.

By the mid 1840s, when Wickliffe's term as postmaster general was coming to an end and a new postmaster was about to be installed, the voices calling for federal postal reform were quite loud and insistent in the land. The Post Office Department itself had grown larger and larger, to the extent that between 1789 and 1845 the number of post offices in the United States had grown from seventy-five to 14,183. More significantly, post office revenues were beginning to pick up again. In 1790, the nation's first full year of operations under the Constitution, postal revenues amounted to $37,935, and expenditures totaled $32,140; and thus there was a profit. But in the nineteenth century, with a larger population and greater distances to cover, there were more years of deficit than profit, especially in the recession years of the 1830s. However, the 1845 figures showed that, while there was still a deficit, it was not as serious as before. The revenues that year amounted to $4,289,842, compared to $4,320,732 in expenditures. In other words, out of a $4 million plus budget, the department was within about $40,000 of breaking even.

Figures of that kind indicated that there might be some flexibility in the system, and that the post office could now afford to lower rates somewhat, in order to make the mails more accessible to greater numbers of people, without suffering ruinous deficits for the Treasury. The mails would still have to be subsidized by the Treasury, of course, but it seemed the Treasury could afford a bit more of a subsidy than it was presently giving.

Apparently even Charles Wickliffe himself, near the end of his tenure, had come around to that viewpoint, and he was then admitting that the reduction of postal rates was possible. But time was running out for him, and he would never supervise a major postal reform during his term in the postmaster general's office. His mentor, President John Tyler, at first decided to run for a second term, but then withdrew his name, and the Whigs nominated Henry Clay. The Democrats in turn nominated James Polk, the first "dark horse" candidate in American history, who then defeated Clay by 170 to 105 electoral votes on December 4, 1844. (Uniform November presidential elections were passed into law by an act of Congress the following year.)

The first two cabinet selections made by the new President-elect were

James Buchanan as secretary of state and Cave Johnson as postmaster general, which is an indication of the importance that the postal question had assumed at the time. Cave Johnson, from Tennessee, was a lawyer and a long-time congressman, and also a confidential friend and advisor to James Polk. The incoming postmaster general, with Polk's backing, announced that he was in favor of an immediate lowering of postal rates.

Sensing the wide public support for reduced postage rates, Congress had been studying the postal question for some months, but with the new administration's strong position on the matter it forged ahead in earnest, even during Wickliffe's remaining time in office, in the first two months of 1845.

∿∿

On January 27, 1845, Senator William Merrick of Maryland introduced a bill to reduce postal rates, saying on the floor of the Senate that the post office was

> *a most important element in the hand of civilization, especially of a republican people. . . . Because it was so well understood by those who framed the Constitution, we find in that sacred instrument that the power of this department of the public service is exclusively vested in Congress. . . . Every nook and corner of this country should be visited by its operations, that it should shed light and information to the remote frontier settler as well as to the inhabitant of the populous city or densely populated districts.*

The bandwagon for postal reform was rolling now, and the flowery rhetoric continued in the Senate, and then passed over to the House. On March 1 of that year Congressman John Paterson of New York spoke of the post office on the floor of the House in roseate terms when he asked, rhetorically, what institution is "so calculated to awaken the ambition of the people to become educated as the cultivation of the taste for epistolatory correspondence, calling into action those energies of the mind so necessary to the intelligent discharge of the high and responsible duties of freedom. . . ."

Finally, on March 3, 1845, the day before Polk was inaugurated, Congress passed a postal reform act which was to become effective on July 1 of that year. By this act, letter rates were, for the first time in America, based on weight, rather than the number of sheets. Furthermore, there would now be only two distance charges—one for distances under 300 miles and another for all distances over that. The half-ounce was the unit weight, and a "single" letter was considered to be one weighing up to one-half ounce. Letters up to a half-ounce cost five cents for 300 miles, and ten cents for any greater distance. There was also a two-cent charge for "drop letters"—that is, mail deposited at the same post office where the recipient picked up the mail and which therefore required no transportation. Packets weighing more than three pounds were not accepted in the mails.

The reduced and simplified postal rates of 1845 were a great step forward, and they were popularly received and widely used. However, they were only a partial reflection of Hill's reforms in England, which had been so warmly endorsed by George Plitt five years earlier. There were still no general issue postage stamps in the United States, and prepayment of the new five- and ten-cent rates was still optional.

On March 4, 1845, James Knox Polk of North Carolina was sworn into office as the nation's eleventh President. The new postmaster general, Cave Johnson, would supervise the new postal rates passed into law the preceding day, but he also had plans for still other postal reforms, including the issuance of a federal adhesive.

IV The Postmasters' Provisionals, 1845–1847

THE FINANCIAL RESULT OF THE 1845 POSTAL REFORMS IN AMERICA was the same as in England: postal revenues dropped. During the first year of the new rates in this country, the loss of revenues resulted in a postal deficit of well over one million dollars.

There was some talk in Congress of trying to prevent this deficit by either curtailing some aspects of postal service or revising the rates of 1845 in order to increase revenues. President Polk, however, had early on made his feelings known regarding postal service finances. In his December 2, 1845, Message to Congress, the fifty-year-old new President said that he felt the postal service should indeed be able to support itself on its own revenues, but that Congress had "never sought to make it a source of revenue except for a short period during the last war with Great Britain." He also said that the expansion of the mail service, particularly on the developing western frontier, "will not admit of such curtailment as will materially reduce the present expenditure."

It was to be the position of both the Polk administration and the Taylor administration which followed it that a complete postal service at the lowest possible rates was something the federal government owed to its citizenry. They preferred to set the rates of postage too low rather than too high, arguing that in this way, greater numbers of people would be able to benefit from the mail service. So the Congress and the executive branch of government remained at a stand-off, and six years were to pass before various conditions necessitated further reform of the rate structure. In the meantime, the simplified rates of 1845—single-letter rates of five cents for under 300 miles and ten cents for over that distance—were encouraging

The five-cent New York postmaster's provisional stamp on this 1847 cover indicated that the postage for a single letter to a destination less than 300 miles away had been paid. Because the provisional stamps were only recognized at the local post office, the cover was marked "PAID" and struck with a New York circular date stamp indicating the postage rate of five cents, just as if the postage had been paid in cash. (National Philatelic Collection)

increased use of the mails. In addition, the simplified rates led to the one of the most interesting postal developments in the history of our country, the "postmasters' provisional" stamps.

The issuance of the stamps we now call postmasters' provisionals was significant for two reasons. First, the stamps are the first instances of United States first-class-letter postage being prepaid by the use of postal adhesives. Second, they were produced entirely on the initiative of local postmasters in a small number of towns, and most of the local issues were produced long before the federal issues which were to follow had been planned. The motivation behind the issue was, of course, money. While it is true that the use of these stamps was not wide, and that most of them were sold at "face value," with no mark-up for production costs, it is also true that the use of the stamps required prepayment, an uncommon practice at this time, and the more money a postmaster collected, the greater was the compensation he received from the Post Office Department. It was the hope of most postmasters who issued their own stamps that either the novelty or convenience of the adhesive labels would lead to a greater increase in the prepayment of postage from their offices, resulting in a higher salary for themselves.

The first of the provisional stamps was issued in New York City on July 14, 1845, just two weeks after the new postal rates went into effect. The postmaster of New York, Robert H. Morris, who had come into office in May of that year, contracted with Rawdon, Wright, Hatch, and Edson, a New York firm specializing in bank-note engraving, to engrave and print the stamps for his office. An invoice delivered to the postmaster on July 12 shows the cost of producing this first stamp:

Postmaster R. H. Morris

1845

July 12	Engraving steel plate of Post Office Stamps,	$40.00
"	Printing 1,000 impressions,	$10.00
"	167 sheets paper and gumming do	$ 5.01
		$55.01

The New York stamps were printed in black on thin paper with a pale bluish tint, or on a somewhat thicker white paper. The design was a portrait of George Washington within a double oval frame. Above the portrait were the words "POST OFFICE," and below it "FIVE CENTS." (It should be remembered that the New York post office's carrier service was at the same time using a city delivery stamp which also showed a portrait of Washington. The three-cent United States City Despatch Post stamp, which we discussed earlier, was not valid for regular first-class-letter postage, only for the carrier service *within* the city.) The new provisional stamps were generally canceled with "PAID" handstamped in red ink, although some copies were struck with the circular "NEW YORK" dated handstamp, or even the octagon-boxed "US" handstamp of the carrier service. The five-cent denomination was the only one issued at New York, and letters which required additional postage, because of weight or a destination more than 300 miles away, are found with two or more copies of the stamp.

On July 12, 1845, Morris wrote identical letters to his fellow postmasters in Boston, Philadelphia, Albany, and Washington, informing them of the issuance of his stamp:

My Dear Sir:—I have adopted a stamp which I sell at 5 cents each. The accompanying is one. I prefer losing the cost of making them to having it insinuated that I am speculating out of the public. Your office of course will not officially notice my stamp, but will be governed by the post office stamp of prepayment. Should there by any accident be deposited at your office a letter directed to the City of New York with one of my stamps upon it, you will mark the letter unpaid the same as though no stamp was upon it, though when it reaches my office I shall deliver it as a paid letter. In this manner the accounts, of the offices will be kept as now, there can be no confusion, and as each office is the judge of its own stamps there will be no danger from counterfeits.

Robt. H. Morris, P.M.

In order to prevent counterfeits of his stamps from passing through the New York office, Postmaster Morris authenticated each of the stamps he sold by signing his initials over the central portrait. When this task became a tedious chore it was delegated to assistants in the post office. Thus we find several sets of initials used to countersign the stamps. From the time of issue until the New York stamps were withdrawn in mid-1847, more than 140,000 copies of the stamp were printed, by far the largest number produced of any provisional.

Another form of the provisionals of the period was the handstamped envelope, such as the one issued by the post office in New Haven, Connecticut, in 1845. Postmaster E.A. Mitchell devised a system whereby his customers

The Providence, Rhode Island, postmaster's provisional stamp. (R. Meyersburg collection)

could bring their own envelopes to the office and he would handstamp them, validating them for five cents of postage per handstamp.

Mitchell had a brass handstamp designed by F.P. Gorham, then the principal engraver in New Haven. Its impression was an upright box which contained in successive lines the words "POSTOFFICE, NEW HAVEN, CT., 5," and "PAID." At the bottom was a line for a signature, followed by the letters "PM." The postmaster stamped the envelopes in red ink and signed his own name in blue ink.

In correspondence, Mitchell noted that "the amount sold were few and probably not over 2,000 all together." He observed that the "object in getting up the stamp was simply to accommodate the public, as I charge no profit." And he stated the obvious convenience the handstamp would afford to his customers: "As no letters could be paid after business hours or Sundays, these were convenient for that purpose as well as others."

Provisionals were found as far west as the Mississippi, such as the stamp issued by the St. Louis, Missouri, post office in November 1845. These stamps are notable because for the first time they feature likenesses other than that of George Washington, and they were also issued in denominations other than five cents.

In the *Missouri Republican* of November 5 this notice was published to announce the new stamps:

LETTER STAMPS.—*Mr. Wimer, the postmaster, has prepared a set of letter stamps, or rather marks, to be put upon letters, indicating that the postage has been paid. In this he has copied after the plan adopted by the postmaster of New York and other cities. These stamps are engraved to represent the Missouri coat of arms, and are five and ten cents. They are so prepared that they may be stuck upon a letter like a wafer and will prove a great convenience to merchants and all those having many letters to send post paid, as it saves all trouble of paying at the post office. They will be sold as they are sold in the East, viz: sixteen five-cent stamps and eight ten-cent stamps for a dollar.*

Here we see that the postmaster is adding a surcharge to the stamps, a hefty one at that, because one dollar purchased only eighty cents worth of either five- or ten-cent stamps. Apparently this charge was considered excessive, and the following week in the same newspaper another notice was printed which lowered the prices, so that the purchaser would receive ninety cents worth of either five- or ten-cent stamps for a dollar.

The illustration on the St. Louis stamp is, as stated in the newspaper notice, the Missouri coat of arms. Across the top of stamp is printed "SAINT LOUIS," then beneath it either the numeral "5" or "10," and at the bottom the words "POST OFFICE." The illustration depicts two bears holding a shield which says "United we stand divided we fall." The two animals are standing on a scroll stating in Latin, "*Salus Populi Suprema Lex*" (The welfare of the people is the supreme law).

Postmaster John Wimer had the plate for the stamps engraved by J.M. Kershaw, a leading St. Louis engraver. The first printing consisted of 500 sheets with only six stamps on each sheet—three each of the five- and ten-cent denominations. The paper for the first printing was greenish gray. The stamps were placed in use in November 1845, and within a few months there grew a demand for stamps of higher denominations for use on bulky business correspondence. A large part of the St. Louis issue was used by two major firms in the city, one a banking house and the other dealing in whole-sale dry goods. There was a steady stream of mail between these two firms and their correspondents in Louisville, Kentucky, and much of this mail was in the form of business contracts and lengthy letters which far exceeded the single-letter weight allowance of one-half ounce. With only five- and ten-cent stamps on hand, these mailings often required several stamps to make up the necessary postage. Thus, in early 1846 some stamps were printed in the twenty-cent denomination. To print these, it was necessary to alter the original plates so that two of the five-cent stamps were changed to twenty-five cent stamps. The St. Louis stamps remained in use until the introduction of the first federal issue in 1847.

Out of the thousands of post offices which serviced mail in the mid-1840s, only twenty to thirty are known to have issued provisional stamps of one sort or another. Some issues, such as the prepaid envelopes of Washington, D.C., are chronicled in the newspapers of the period, but have never been seen by modern collectors. The stamps and prepaid envelopes issued by Postmaster, later President, James Buchanan of Baltimore, Maryland, are quite scarce even though Baltimore was then a busy commercial center.

The provisional stamp issued by Postmaster Frederick N. Palmer of Brattleboro, Vermont, was a simple rectangular design featuring the name of the post office and the postmaster's initials.

Palmer was a music teacher who also ran the post office, and in the summer of 1846 he issued a small edition of 500 five-cent stamps, the plate for which had been engraved for him by Thomas Chubbuck of Brattleboro. Some years later Chubbuck was interviewed for an article which appeared in the November 1870 issue of the *Stamp Collector's Record*, published in Albany , New York, and in the interview he recalled that the main reason why Palmer issued the stamps was "to turn an honest penny." The postmaster's salary, Chubbuck maintained, was proportionate to the cash receipts of his office, and it was in the postmaster's best financial interests to have as many letters as possible prepaid in Brattleboro. Palmer hoped that the novelty and convenience of the new stamps would encourage their sale, and he even offered to sell them on credit. That the novelty of the stamps did help to boost sales is proven by the notation inside one of the few Brattleboro provisional covers known to us today: "I pay this just to shew [sic] the stamp. It is against my principles you know."

Only a small number of the original 500 stamps were apparently sold in the small town of Brattleboro, however, during the twelve months they were valid, and Chubbuck recalls that Palmer burned the remaining stamps in July 1847, when the first federal issue became available. The torching of a small batch of postmaster's provisional stamps in Brattleboro, Vermont, was a fitting symbolic end to the short period during which these local issues saw service. The utility of the postal adhesive had now been proven in America, and the glow from the burning pile of stamps in Vermont heralded the introduction of the first United States government postage stamp.

V *The First Federal-Issue Postage Stamps, 1847*

CAVE JOHNSON WAS FIFTY-TWO YEARS OLD WHEN HE WAS APPOINTED postmaster general by President Polk in 1845, and he possessed precisely the qualities needed to keep postal reform on the move in Washington, where many congressmen were saying that the 1845 reforms were enough, and indeed may well have been too much.

As a young man he had served as a lieutenant in the Tennessee militia, fighting against the Creek Indians under Gen. Andrew Jackson in 1813 and 1814. After studying law under William Cooks, Johnson was elected prosecuting attorney in 1817. He was elected as a Democrat to the Twenty-first Congress, and was reelected three succeeding times, serving in Washington from 1829 to 1837. Johnson was defeated in the 1836 election, but he was returned to the next three congresses, from 1839 to 1845.

During his fourteen years in Washington, Cave Johnson had acquired a reputation for unusual skill in managerial affairs and political maneuvering, and he was recognized as a man who knew his way around the corridors of power in the nation's capital. James Polk was aware of these qualities when he appointed him to the sensitive position of postmaster general in 1845. Furthermore, Johnson had one other invaluable asset in Washington: he was a close friend and confidant of the new President.

The first year of Johnson's term was spent in supervising the new postal reforms of 1845, and then he had to defend those reforms against the congressmen who wanted to rescind some of them when revenues dropped dramatically. Thus when he began to lobby for further reforms in 1846 he met with a considerable amount of opposition from some members of Congress. Johnson would like to have implemented the entire Plitt report from the

Cave Johnson, postmaster general, 1845–1849.

last Democratic administration with the full postal plan enacted in England, but being a political realist he had to settle for only what he thought possible in Congress in 1846 and 1847: the issuance of a federal postage stamp.

Even at that, it was a difficult struggle for Johnson, and his announcement that the Post Office Department wanted to issue a stamp was not met with universal enthusiasm in Congress. During the first year of the new postal reforms the department was already suffering a severe deficit, and now Johnson wanted to issue a stamp which would be sold at face value and thus incur to the post office the additional cost of manufacturing the stamps. Johnson argued that the convenience of the stamps would increase the use of the mails and thus postal revenues. He also pointed out that in England, during the early years of its postal reforms, there had been quite serious deficits, but now revenues were increasing remarkably and by 1846, just six years after beginning, mail in England had almost quadrupled.

Then there was some general mistrust in Congress of the very idea of a postage stamp itself. People were not generally interested in *prepaying* for any service, some congressmen said, echoing the same sentiments stated during the debate over the postal reforms in England. But if people did want to prepay they always could do so without an adhesive label, and now there were even a number of postmasters who were issuing their own stamps. Let the postmasters continue to issue stamps if they wanted, but it was not the role of the federal government. Johnson, the old Washington hand, had to contend with these arguments, pointing out that the postage stamp was the thing of the future and that more and more countries were using them. He also had to argue against another frequently stated fear about postage stamps: that they could be counterfeited and the mails thus used for free. Johnson answered that the use of detailed engravings by superior craftsmen should minimize that problem—and in that he was largely correct.

To Johnson's credit, he lobbied Congress successfully, and a postal act was passed into law on March 3, 1847, authorizing a federal postage stamp. The new act read in part:

> *And be it further enacted, that to facilitate the transportation of letters by mail, the Postmaster General be authorized to prepare postage stamps, which when attached to any letter or packet, shall be evidence of prepayment of the postage chargeable on such letter.*

The act would go into effect on July 1, 1847, and it prohibited the postmasters from issuing any local stamps from that date. But Cave Johnson recognized that the new act had a serious flaw, namely that the new stamps would not be compulsory, which meant that many of the old subterfuges for avoiding the payment of postage could still continue. The optional nature of the stamps authorized in 1847 would also mean, as we shall see, that they were underused and that the general issue of 1847 was actually "general" in name only.

Throughout the four years of his term as postmaster general, Johnson would continue to argue unsuccessfully for an obligatory stamp, and in the Postmaster General's Report of 1848 he stated that "all matter sent in the mails should be prepaid." In that same report, he noted that nearly two million dead letters without postage are not claimed each year, which meant

Proof impressions of the dies for the first federal postage stamp issue of 1847. The crosshatching around the stamp designs was not transferred to the actual printing plate. (National Philatelic Collection)

that the post office had carried them without any reimbursement. He added that a similar number of newspapers and periodicals which had been mailed to post offices went unclaimed each year, and in New York alone there were 52,000 of these unclaimed periodicals annually.

Nevertheless, Cave Johnson had achieved one important thing in 1847: the first United States federal postage stamp.

Johnson contracted with the bank-note firm of Rawdon, Wright, Hatch, and Edson, which, as we noted, produced the New York postmaster's stamp in

1845, and which was located in New York City on the top floor of a building at the corner of William and Wall streets. The firm was instructed to produce two stamps: a five-cent stamp bearing the portrait of Benjamin Franklin and a ten-cent stamp bearing George Washington's likeness. There has been some discussion as to why Johnson selected Franklin's portrait rather than Washington's on the primary five-cent stamp, which would undoubtedly receive wider usage, and the answer seems to be because Franklin was considered in some quarters as the "father" of the American Postal Service.

Neither of the two portraits was specially commissioned for the stamp issue; both were stock portrait dies which the engraving firm possessed and which had been used previously on bank notes. The Franklin portrait had been painted by James B. Longacre, a well-known artist. The Washington portrait is the famous one by Stuart. The five-cent stamp featured the portrait of Franklin in an oval frame, the words "FIVE CENTS" under the oval, and the numeral "5" in both lower corners. The lettering on the ten-cent stamp was the same, except for the different denominations, but it is curious that on the Franklin stamp the arabic numeral "5" is used, while the Washington stamp bears the roman numeral "X."

These stamps were issued in sheets of 100 each, without perforations, and they had to be cut apart for use. The five-cent stamp was printed in brown on a bluish woven paper, but it appeared in a variety of shades; the ten-cent stamp appears in black, gray-black, and greenish-black. (These various shades of the stamps were not, of course, part of the original printing, but they were done in subsequent printings during the years the stamps were valid, as will be the case in the shades of the stamps to be discussed

The five-cent rate for single letters going less than 300 miles was prepaid with a five-cent Franklin postage stamp on this 1849 cover from Washington City, D.C., to Bentivoglio, Virginia, a small town near Charlottesville. The envelope was addressed to William C. Rives, an eminent statesman of the nineteenth century who served in Congress and as minister to France. (National Philatelic Collection)

throughout the book.) Both stamps measured eighteen and one-half by twenty-three and one-quarter millimeters.

There has been some controversy in the history of philately about the type of metal used for the plates for the 1847 stamps, but Lester Brookman in his monumental *The United States Postage Stamps of the 19th Century* is of the opinion that the plates were made of steel. Brookman also notes that nearly every extant ten-cent stamp of that issue is of good, sharp impression, while very few of the five-cent stamps "can be rated as better than fair to poor." He then concludes that the reason for the many unclear impres-

The single-letter rate for mail going more than 300 miles was paid with a single ten-cent Washington stamp of the 1847 issue on this cover from St. Louis to Boston. (R. Meyersburg collection)

sions on the five-cent stamp was because of the quality of the ink and "indifferent printing."

The 1847 postage stamps were produced by a process known as line engraving, which was used for all American postage stamps for the remainder of the century. Here is a brief description of the process:

Making the die. The initial step in line engraving is to make the die,

The 1847 issue did not include denominations in the rates for carrier and drop-letter services, but some postmasters, with the blessing of the Post Office Department, produced stamps for use by the carrier service operating in their cities. This cover bears a copy of the New York "lifesaver" carrier stamp (black on buff paper), paying the fee for carrier service to the mails, and a five-cent 1847 postage stamp prepaying the single-letter rate to Elizabethtown, New Jersey. Carrier services are discussed further in chapter 7. (R. Meyersburg collection)

which is a small, flat piece of metal—usually soft steel—about three and one-half inches square and about one-quarter to three-quarter inches thick. The design desired for the stamp is cut in mirror image into the steel by the engraver. The die is then hardened, usually by heating it in a bath of cyanide of potassium and then dipping it in cold oil.

The transfer roll. This is the step which makes possible the transfer of the design from the die to the plate. The die is placed against the transfer roll, which is a roll of soft steel shaped like a small grindstone, and enormous hand-lever pressure is used to press the die against the roll. The result of that operation is that every line that has been cut in the dies now stands *up* in relief on the face of the transfer roll—and we then have what is called a "relief," which is hardened in the same manner as the die had been.

The plate. The plates used in the production of nineteenth-century American stamps were usually made of soft steel, about a quarter of an inch thick, and they were large enough to accommodate 200 positions for stamp impressions. The hardened transfer roll was placed against the plate, and pressed against it, which entered the design on the plate. This process was repeated again and again across the plate, one entry for each stamp desired.

Printing. To prepare the plate for printing, ink is then worked onto the plate with a roller or a dabber, so that the surface is thoroughly covered. After the ink has been worked into all of the lines in the plate, the printer removes the surplus from the surface with a cloth. The paper to be used for the stamp impressions is moistened so that it can better take the ink from the plate, and it is then placed on the inked plate. Plate and paper are next rolled under a blanket cylinder, which forces the fibers of the paper down into the lines of the plate, causing the transfer of the ink from the plate to the paper. The printed sheet is then carefully removed from the plate, and the result is a sheet of stamps.

Adhesives. Placing the adhesive material on the back of the sheet is a far less technical and skillful process than the printing described above. For the 1847 stamps produced by Rawdon, Wright, Hatch and Edson, the firm used a yellow gum which was applied by an apprentice engraver and an apprentice printer. These two apprentices, in addition to their regular duties, were employed as watchmen, and three nights a week they gummed the sheets of newly printed stamps and hung them up about the room to dry.

Such was the process which produced those first federal stamps of 1847.

∿∿

The new stamps were to become valid on July 1, according to the congressional act, but, because of production delays at the printing firm in New York, probably only one post office actually had them on hand by that date— the post office in New York. Boston received a supply on the following day, and by the end of the month a number of other post offices had the new issue.

According to postal legend, the first actual purchase of stamps from the new issue was made in the office of Cave Johnson in Washington by Representative Harvey Shaw of New York. A recollective article which appeared in the *Hartford Times* of August 5, 1885, relates that the congressman was visiting the postmaster general's office when the stamps were first delivered by the printer. Johnson laid the sheets of stamps on his desk, and after giving his receipt for them, handed one sheet to Shaw to inspect. "Mr. Shaw returned them after a hasty glance, and then drawing out his wallet, he counted out fifteen cents, with which he purchased two of the stamps—the first two ever issued." Congressman Shaw reportedly kept the five-cent stamp "as a curiosity," and gave the other to the governor of Connecticut.

From the first deliveries of 1847 until December 9, 1850, some 4,400,000 five-cent stamps and 1,050,000 ten-cent stamps were delivered to the Post Office Department by the printer. However, only 3,712,000 five-cent and

Local dispatch and delivery companies continued to operate in direct competition with the post office even after the introduction of the first federal stamps. This cover, bearing a one-cent stamp of Blood's Philadelphia Dispatch Company, was carried outside the mails to the Philadelphia railroad terminal where it was put on a train bound for New York. At New York the cover entered the U.S. postal system, and the five-cent postage stamp, paying the rate to Providence, Rhode Island, was canceled and the New York circular marking applied. By using a private dispatch service to carry the letter directly to the railroad terminal, the sender was able to speed his message on its way, saving at least a day over the normal postal transit. (R. Meyersburg collection)

891,000 ten-cent stamps were actually distributed to individual postmasters. These figures represent the total number of the 1847 issue printed and distributed, because the issue was demonetized in 1851 when new rates went into effect and new stamps were issued. The small number printed and the still smaller number actually distributed during those five years indicate the rather limited use of the 1847 issue.

The stamps were used mainly in the more populous and well-settled areas along the Atlantic coast, particularly the northern states, and in the

Some of the steamboats which carried mail during the 1840s were under contract to the Post Office Department, but other vessels also carried mail along their routes. The captains of these "noncontract" boats were compensated for carrying the mail at a rate of two cents per letter. The boxed "TROY & NEW YORK STEAM BOAT" marking on this cover indicates that it was carried by a noncontract steamer. This is the only cover bearing this marking which does not show an additional handstamped mark indicating the two-cent credit to the captain. Letters carried on noncontract vessels were charged the regular letter rates even though the post office paid a greater part of its receipts for their transport. (R. Meyersburg collection)

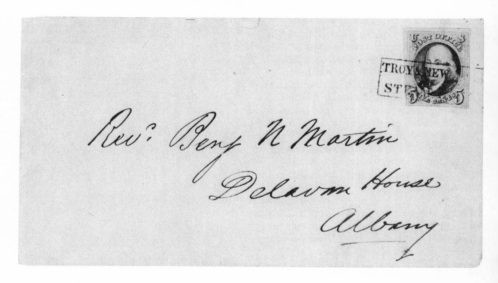

areas of the Ohio and Mississippi river basins. There was some use of the 1847 issue in California and in western territories such as Wisconsin, Oregon, New Mexico, and even in the Indian Territory, the region to which several eastern American Indian tribes had been forcibly relocated early in the nineteenth century.

Some of the most interesting usages of the issue of 1847 are those found from the U.S. Mail Dispatch Agency at Panama in Central America. Other outstanding usages occurred when correspondence from Canada was franked with United States stamps in order to pay the postage required from the border to a destination within this country. At that time Canada had not yet issued its first postage stamps and the Canadian postage on these rare foreign uses of the United States stamps was usually paid in cash by the sender.

As Cave Johnson had predicted, the stamps did to some extent encourage wider use of the mails, or at least more prepayment of postal fees. Mail users who were already in the practice of prepaying their letters found the stamps to be a great convenience. The novelty of using these new stamps is quaintly expressed in the footnote to a February 22, 1848, letter from Theodore Harris of Newbury, Massachusetts, to his mother in Portsmouth, New Hampshire:

> *I shall pay for this letter by sticking a "stamp" on it, don't you think we had better buy a few at the Post Office, they are real handy, no trouble about stopping at the Post Office to pay, and they have something on the back which sticks to the letter by wetting.*

While the postmaster general had also been correct in his assumption that intricate engraving on the new stamps would discourage any attempts to make counterfeits, a minor problem was discovered to be the practice of some postal patrons who "cleaned" stamps which had already been used, washing off the cancellation so that the stamp could be used again. This was not a widespread problem, although in later years the Post Office Department spent considerable effort in attempts to prevent the reuse by encouraging the development of elaborate "security printing" processes, which we will discuss later.

One noteworthy practice, which developed soon after the new stamps were introduced, was the bisecting of stamps so that a lesser amount of postage was paid than the stamp's value indicated. This practice never received the official blessing of the Post Office Department, but some postmasters found that half of a ten-cent stamp worked just as well as a five-cent stamp when the lower value was not available. It is also possible that the five-cent stamp could be found in a legitimate bisected use. The postmaster of New York, for example, in an advertisement in *The Evening Post* of January 5, 1850, posted a notice that he would accept half of a five-cent stamp as payment for picking up a newspaper which had not been prepaid. "This arrangement will obviate the necessity of a great deal of delay at the post office windows in the payment of newspaper postage."

∿∿

We have no reliable records of how many of the stamps from this first federal issue were actually sold to the public. When the stamps were demonetized in 1851, local postmasters were given a short time during which the 1847 issue could be redeemed for either cash or the new issue of stamps. Brookman estimates that of the 891,000 ten-cent stamps actually distributed to postmasters, some 865,000 were sold to the public. Even at that, the 1847 issue stamps represented only a small portion of the postal transactions for the years 1847–51. Although there were some 17,437 post offices by the year 1851, only a small handful actually received the stamps for use. During

On this cover the five-cent stamp is tied by a circular "HUDSON RIVER MAIL N.Y." handstamp, indicating that the letter was carried by a boat operating under contract to the post office. The captains of contract vessels did not receive the two-cent-per-letter fee, but they did get paid for the mail they carried according to the terms of their post office contract. (R. Meyersburg collection)

those years, the total Post Office Department receipts for all mail, including both prepaid and letters with the postage due upon receipt, was roughly $15,500,000. At the same time, the face value of all of the 1847 stamps distributed to post offices—and deducting nothing for those copies never sold to the public—was $274,700 ($185,600 in five-cent stamps and $89,100 in ten-cent stamps). Thus, the *face value* of all of those stamps constituted less than 2 percent of the actual postage which was collected during the

The two ten-cent stamps on this cover paid the postage for a quadruple-weight letter going less than 300 miles. The cover, mailed at Philadelphia, contained several business contracts and receipts for Charles Potter, a wealthy merchant in Providence, Rhode Island. (National Philatelic Collection)

years that they were valid.

Cave Johnson, therefore, had been right to complain that the stamps needed to be compulsory in order to be truly effective. The 1847 issue was a great historic development on the American scene, but rather than its classification as the first *general issue* of postage stamps, as it has been frequently called, this may be more accurately described as the first *federal issue* of adhesive postage stamps.

VI The Stamp Comes of Age in America, 1851–1856

THE YEARS 1849 AND 1850 WERE ONES OF POLITICAL CONFUSION IN Washington, because during those two years there were three Presidents, and consequently three postmasters general. James Polk was finishing his first term in 1848, and although it was a successful one as judged by historical standards, he had not been well liked in Washington, and furthermore his health was failing. He had decided not to seek renomination, completing his term on March 5, 1849. Three months later he died at the age of fifty-four. Postmaster Cave Johnson went out of office with Polk, returning to his native Tennessee where he practiced law and then became president of the State Bank of Tennessee.

In the presidential election of 1848, the Whigs were returned to power with the election of one of the heroes of the Mexican War, Gen. Zachary Taylor, and his running mate, Millard Filmore. In assembling his cabinet, Taylor appointed Jacob Collamer, a lawyer from Vermont and three-term congressman, as his postmaster general. Although Collamer was later to have a long and distinguished career as a senator from Vermont, his tenure as postmaster general was brief and unmemorable because of Taylor's short presidency. On July 4, 1850, just sixteen months into his term, Taylor attended a ceremony in Washington connected with the building of the Washington monument, and he became overheated and drank large amounts of ice water. That evening he had a raging fever and was diagnosed as having "cholera morbus." Five days later Taylor was dead at the age of sixty-five.

Taylor was succeeded by his vice-president, Millard Fillmore of New York, and, according to the custom of the time, Taylor's entire cabinet resigned to allow the new President to choose his own members. For the position of postmaster general, Fillmore chose one of his old legal associates, Nathan Hall of New York. As a young man Hall had entered the law office of a struggling young lawyer in Aurora, New York, Millard Fillmore. After he had been admitted to the bar, he formed a partnership with Fillmore in Buffalo, which lasted for ten years. In 1841 Hall became a judge in the court of common pleas, and in 1847 he was elected to the House of Representatives as a Whig. He was forty-two years old in 1850 when Fillmore appointed him postmaster general.

Nathan Hall has been described as an intensely serious, almost austere personality, with a fervent dedication to the principles of law and ethics. He brought this spirit of absolute equity and justice with him to the job of postmaster general as he viewed the postal situation in America in the new decade of the 1850s. One of the first things to confront him was the continuing clamor for further postal reform, and Hall agreed with the logic of the proponents of reform that there were inequities involved in the present rates. A.D. Smith, in *The Development of Rates of Postage*, notes that at that time the regular charge for transporting a barrel of flour from Detroit to Buffalo was ten cents, the same charge that was levied by the government for carrying a letter weighing a half-ounce.

Hall began to lobby Congress for new postal reforms, experiencing some of the same resistance that Cave Johnson had encountered before him, but he was successful in obtaining the postal act of March 3, 1851, which if it did not implement all the elements of the Plitt report eleven years earlier, at least took it as far as the next-to-last step. The act of 1851 established what were for all practical purposes uniform rates for domestic letters. On

Nathan Hall, postmaster general, 1850–1852

the other hand, the act still did not make prepayment compulsory, but it did make it attractive. The rate for unpaid single letters would still be five cents, but if prepaid, the rate would be only three cents. This reduced rate meant that in 1851 there would be a need for a new issue of stamps.

〜〜〜

The act of 1851 was to become effective on July 1 of that year, and it contained a number of new elements:

* The charge for every single letter—that is, less than one-half ounce—was to be three cents, if prepaid, for distances up to 3,000 miles. For every additional half ounce an additional single-letter charge would be made.

* Letters not prepaid would be charged five cents, according to the same scale as above.

* For distances over 3,000 miles the above rates were doubled.

* Drop letters—those left at a post office to be picked up at the same office by the recipient—would be charged one cent.

* "Advertised letters" would be charged one cent in addition to the regular postage. (These were letters not claimed at the post office, and which were listed in the local newspapers by the postmaster. The extra one-cent fee covered the advertising costs.)

* A charge of one cent for unsealed circulars of one ounce or less sent for distances of less than 500 miles. (The following year, the act of August 30, 1852, amended those rates so that the one-cent rate was allowed for circulars of up to three ounces sent anywhere in the country.)

* The act also defined the counterfeiting of stamps as a "felony" and

The three-cent stamp on this cover can be identified as coming from the early state of plate one; stamps from this early state of the plate are found used only during 1851, thus making this Philadelphia cover an example of second-day use of the issue, July 2, 1851. (R. Meyersburg collection)

OPPOSITE: *The primary use of the one-cent stamp of 1851 was the payment of postage on printed circulars and drop letters, although that denomination is also found making up other rates. This outstanding cover bears a strip of five, a block of four, and a single one-cent stamp which, supplementing the ten-cent stamped envelope, paid the twenty-cent postage rate for a double-weight letter from Strawberry Valley, California, to Mobile, Alabama. (R. Meyersburg collection)*

provided for penalties of a fine of $500 or five years' imprisonment or both.

* Finally, the act said that the postmaster general should provide "suitable postage stamps of the denomination of three cents, and such other denominations as he may think expedient to facilitate prepayment of postages provided in this act."

In compliance with the act and because the new one-cent and three-cent

The postmaster in the small town of Cloverport, Kentucky, frequently made new handstamp devices for use in his office. More than thirteen different markings from this small office have been recorded for the period from 1847 to 1861. This November 1851 cover has the only known strike of the large oval marking with negative lettering. It is thought that the canceling device for this mark was fashioned from part of the leg bone of a cow, the lettering being carved into the end of a smoothly cut cross section. The envelope is addressed to Joseph Holt, later a postmaster general (1859–60) and secretary of war in 1861. (National Philatelic Collection)

stamps would be immediately needed, Nathan Hall quickly proceeded to arrange for a new printing contract. He awarded the contract to Toppan, Carpenter, Casilear & Co., a firm whose main office and manufacturing facilities were in Philadelphia, although it had branch offices in New York, Boston, and Cincinnati.

The selection of Toppan, Carpenter, and Casilear to replace the firm which had printed the 1847 issue was based on the lower price and higher quality the new firm was able to offer. Thus we find that Nathan Hall, writing in his "Report of the Postmaster General" of November 15 of that year, clearly states that the new stamps of 1851 "are believed to be of superior quality, and are furnished at a less price than was formerly paid." The contract with the firm of Toppan, Carpenter, and Casilear in 1851 was for six years, but it was later extended for another four years, until June 10, 1861.

There were some new features in the 1851 postage stamp contract. For one thing, it provided for the first time a government agent who would be in charge of the dies and plates while they were being used by the printer. When the dies and plates were not being so used, they were to be deposited at the assistant U.S. treasurer's office in Philadelphia until a new run of stamps was ordered. These provisions seem to be based on the continuing fear of misuse of these original plates, which would be even more dangerous than counterfeiting.

Another provision of the new contract was also based on the same apprehension. It provided that the original plates would become the property of the United States government when there were no more orders for that particular issue or when it had been demonetized. This clause would now

This cover, mailed on August 12, 1851, is an example of contract steamboat mail, carried on the Louisville and Cincinnati Mail Line, which ran along the Ohio River. (National Philatelic Collection)

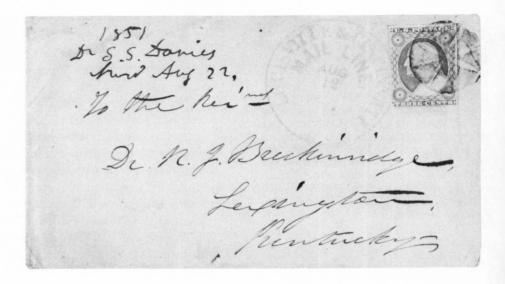

appear in all postage stamp printing contracts up to the time when the government began printing its own stamps at the Bureau of Engraving in 1894. This provision had not been inserted in the 1847 contract with Rawdon, Wright, Hatch and Edson, and in 1851, when those stamps were being demonetized, there was some concern in Washington that the New York firm still retained the original plates. However, Nathan Hall exerted his influence and persuaded the firm to destroy those plates. In Hall's report of November 15, 1851, he noted that "directions for the destruction of the dies and plates employed in the manufacture of the postage stamps formerly used have been given."

The first stamps of the 1851 issue were delivered to the government by Toppan, Carpenter, and Casilear on June 21, 1851, in sheets of imperforate stamps which had to be cut apart by hand. Delivered that day were: 100,000 one-cent stamps, 300,000 three-cent stamps, and 100,000 twelve-cent stamps. The one-cent stamp, of course, was to be used for drop mail and circulars; the three-cent stamp for single letters under 3,000 miles; and the twelve-cent stamp was a quadruple of the basic postage, for use on heavier mail and foreign letters.

Two things should be noted about this 1851 issue. First, the phrase *Issue of 1851* is used in philatelic literature to include all the United States postage stamps issued between 1851 and 1856. As we shall see, some of the stamps of the "1851" issue were actually issued in subsequent years. We shall follow that usual designation, and thus all the stamps in this chapter represent that issue of 1851, even though some of them were issued later than the calendar year of 1851.

Second, it is usual for philatelists to classify these stamps according to "types." For each of the stamps produced in this issue there were die and plate production idiosyncrasies which resulted in stamps showing minor differences in their design. At a later point there were often "reentries" and "recutting" of parts of the plate, which resulted in further variations in the stamps produced. As an example, there are seven "types" of the 1851 one-

The circular "EASTERN R.R." marking indicates that this September 1851 cover was carried to Boston aboard a train run by that small New England rail company. (R. Meyersburg collection)

OPPOSITE: *All mail from Galveston, Texas, was carried by boats because the town is located on an island. This cover has a straight-line "STEAMBOAT" marking to indicate how it was carried to Houston on the nearby Texas shore. (R. Meyersburg collection)*

cent stamp, with the only complete design, type one, being found in only one position on the first plate produced. The types and varieties of these stamps are of great importance and interest to philatelic scholars, but they are beyond the scope of this book, and we here indicate only the basic designs of the 1851 issue:

One cent. A profile bust of Benjamin Franklin on an oval disk, with the words "U.S. POSTAGE" above and "ONE CENT" below. Color, indigo blue.

Three cents. A profile bust of George Washington, after a portrait by Jean Antoine Houdon, on an oval disk. The same lettering, except for the words "THREE CENTS." On this attractive stamp, Washington's portrait is set in a beautifully tesselated (mosaic) frame, and there is a fine lathework rosette in each of the corners. Color, brick red.

Five cents. (This stamp of the "1851" issue was actually issued in 1856 to pay for registered mail, as will be discussed in the next chapter.) A portrait of Thomas Jefferson, after a painting by Stuart, on an oval disk with the words "FIVE CENTS" at the bottom. The oval is set in a four-sided oblong frame which is filled with two rows of geometric lathework. Color, brown.

Ten cents. (This stamp was issued in 1855 to comply with the act of 1855, which established a ten-cent charge for all letters mailed over 3,000 miles, as will be discussed below.) A portrait of George Washington, after the Stuart painting, on an oval disk with the words "TEN CENTS" at the bottom. Around the upper portion of the medallion are thirteen white stars, and the whole is surrounded by highly ornate scrollwork. Color, dark green.

Twelve cents. A portrait of George Washington, after the Stuart painting, on an oval disk with the words "TWELVE CENTS" below. The oval is enclosed in a handsome tesselated frame, with a lathework rosette in each corner. Color, black.

Beginning in 1853, the Post Office Department also issued stamped en-

The "U.S. EXPRESS MAIL N. YORK N.Y."
marking, which cancels the three-cent
stamp on this cover, does not indicate the
same type of service as the express mail
cover shown on page 21. In the 1850s,
markings of this type were applied to mail
carried on the main rail route from New
York to Boston. (R. Meyersburg collection)

velopes with a design featuring a portrait of George Washington. At first, only three- and six-cent envelopes were produced, but a ten-cent envelope was introduced in 1855 to meet the new ten-cent rates. These envelopes are studied in detail by modern philatelists, and there are many types and varieties of each value. In the course of this book, we will not cover the stamped envelope issues in detail, although their uses were the same as for the postage stamps of the period.

Even with the low domestic postage rates in effect in both Britain and the United States in the mid-nineteenth century, some people felt that there was a great need for cheap international rates. This envelope, with its elaborate, engraved design promoting "one penny ocean postage," was printed in London, but used in Philadelphia in the early 1850s. The reverse side of the envelope is pictured here; the front is on the opposite page. (National Philatelic Collection)

Nathan Hall was the sponsor of that 1851 issue, but he was not to be the postmaster general during the entire period of its use because he only remained in office for a little over two years. Millard Fillmore had experienced a stormy time as President, encountering dissatisfaction with his administration from both his own party and the opposition. He was unable to gain the nomination for a second term during the Whig convention of 1852 and the lame-duck President—who was, in fact, to be the last Whig President in American history—then set about doing what he could for his friends.

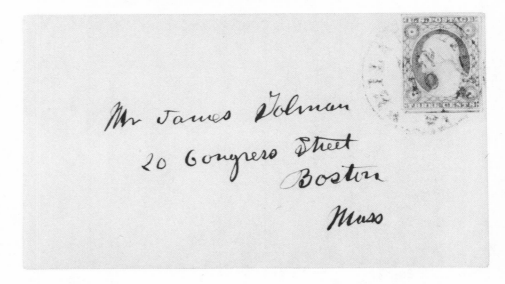

On August 31, 1852, Fillmore appointed Nathan Hall to be United States judge of the Northern District of New York, a position he would hold until his death in 1874. To serve during the last few months of his administration as postmaster general, Fillmore appointed Samuel Hubbard of Connecticut, who would have a brief and unremembered tenure.

In the national election of 1852, the New Hampshire Democrat Franklin Pierce was easily elected President, and he appointed as his postmaster general James Campbell of Philadelphia, who had been extremely active in

The three-cent stamp of 1851, generally used for satisfying the single-letter rate for less than 3,000 miles, is sometimes found in blocks and strips used to pay the higher rates to foreign countries. This cover bears a block of eight three-cent stamps which paid the twenty-four-cent rate for a half-ounce letter to Britain, via British mail service. The postal agreement between the United States and Britain provided for the postage to be shared between the two countries. In the case of this February 2, 1854, cover, five cents were retained by the U.S. post office, and the remaining nineteen cents were credited to Britain—sixteen cents for transatlantic ship and three cents for British inland postage. This cover was recently discovered in the family correspondence of the addressee by the current owner. A valentine was the original enclosure. (R. Meyersburg collection)

local politics. Campbell, a lawyer, had served as school commissioner, and had been appointed judge of the court of common pleas before he was thirty, sitting on that bench for ten years. He was occupying the position of Pennsylvania attorney general when the presidential campaign of 1852 started, and he offered some valuable and unexpected service to the Democratic candidate, which brought him to Pierce's attention. James Campbell was an Irish Catholic and the best-known leader of the Catholic Democrats of Philadelphia at a time when Know-Nothing anti-Catholic prejudice was running high. During the 1852 campaign Pierce was accused of harboring Know-Nothing prejudices against Catholics, and Campbell, with his impeccable credentials, rose to Pierce's defense, denying those charges and rallying the Catholic vote for Pierce. The newly elected President did not forget, and he brought Campbell to Washington with him.

James Campbell was a colorful figure during his four years in Washington as postmaster general, the highest office he would ever hold. At forty-two, he was described as a "fat jolly man," who brought a considerable amount of ebullience and enthusiasm to his job. But despite all of the man's conviviality, he was no fool, and he proved to be an extremely hard worker who was determined to increase the efficiency of the Post Office Department. He was also interested in further postal reform, and accordingly the new Congress started work on a bill which would take the United States postal service that one last step it desperately needed to take.

That act was passed on March 3, 1855, and it was promulgated by James Campbell on March 12 in a proclamation entitled "Instructions to Postmasters." The postal regulations contained in the proclamation were to go into

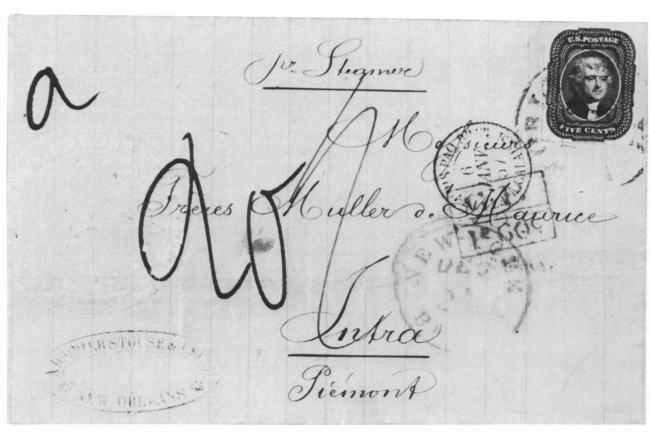

From the first of January until the first of April, 1857, the transatlantic postage rates between the United States and Britain and France were in a confused state. The British and French had just inaugurated a new postal treaty which put the American packet-boat lines in the unfortunate position of being the most expensive method of sending mail to France via England. At the same time, United States postal authorities were negotiating a treaty with France which would make the handling of mail between the two countries both more effective and less expensive. Rather than risk a breakdown of the negotiations with France, the United States was willing to endure the new rates between Britain and France for a short time. During this three-month period, only five American packets and sixteen British Cunard Line sailings occurred. This cover, franked with a five-cent stamp of the 1851 issue, was mailed at New Orleans, and left New York on the first ship to sail after the change of rates, the Cunard Line's Africa. *When the cover arrived at Liverpool on January 6, 1857, it was sent to London, where it was marked with a boxed "G.B. 1F 60C" marking, indicating a credit to France. The cover traveled to Paris by way of Calais, and was then sent on to Italy, where the postage for all services beyond the United States border was collected. (R. Meyersburg collection)*

effect very quickly on April 1 of that year. A single rate would be put into effect for all letters sent under 3,000 miles: three cents for single letters, with the usual multiples for extra weight. For mail over 3,000 miles, the charge would be ten cents, and Campbell stated that "postage stamps and stamped envelopes of the denomination of ten cents will be prepared and issued speedily." Thus there was a need for this denomination again, and the ten-cent stamp described earlier in this chapter was issued in 1855. But the most significant part of Campbell's notice was contained in these words:

That from or after April 1, 1855, pre-payment, either by stamps, stamped envelopes or money, is compulsory.

Prepayment of postage would now be mandatory, starting within a few weeks, although people would still be allowed to pay this charge in cash, without using stamps if they wished. Then Campbell took that final step:

That from and after January 1, 1856, all letters between places in the United States must be pre-paid, either by postage stamps, or stamped envelopes.

There it was: the postage stamp would become obligatory in America on the first day of 1856, some nine months away. At long last, and long overdue, some fifteen years after the Plitt report, all the elements of the Hill plan from England were now in place in America—reduced postage rates, a uniform rate based on weight, and a general issue and compulsory postage stamp. The American postage stamp had come of age.

This cover, mailed at St. Anthony's Falls, Minnesota Territory, on April 23, 1857, has a ten-cent stamp of the 1851 issue paying the rate for letters to Canada. When the cover reached the exchange office at Detroit, it was struck with an oval marking reading "UNITED STATES 6D" and a straight-line "PAID." These markings indicated that the Canadian postage rate of six pence had been paid as a part of the United States charge, and the letter was sent on to its destination at St. Catherine's, Canada West, without further charge. (National Philatelic Collection)`

James Campbell, postmaster general, 1853–1857

The pair of ten-cent stamps on this cover paid the postage on a one-ounce letter from San Francisco to Sherbourne, New York. Stamps of this issue are rarely found with such wide and even margins as on this pair. (R. Meyersburg collection)

Per Cunard Steamer
U.S. POSTAGE
TWELVE CENTS
U.S. POSTAGE
TWELVE CENTS
Robert Charleton.
Ashley Down
Bristol.
England.
JUN
56

On this December 1851 cover from New Orleans, we see the same transatlantic service out of Boston. In this case the letter required double-weight postage, paid with a strip of four twelve-cent stamps, and thirty-eight cents was the credit to Britain. (National Philatelic Collection)

OPPOSITE: The twenty-four-cent rate to Britain was usually paid with two twelve-cent stamps, as we see on this cover from Skaneateles, New York, to Bristol, England. The manuscript notation "per Cunard Steamer" indicated that the letter was to be carried by British packet, resulting in a nineteen-cent credit to Britain, while the United States retained five cents for inland postage. The British incoming foreign mail office at Liverpool struck a circular "America/ Liverpool/ Paid 15 Ju 56" mark directly over the original town handstamp, indicating the origin and payment status of the letter. (R. Meyersburg collection)

The postal act of March 3, 1851, had set the rate for prepaid single letters going more than 3,000 miles at six cents. The 1851 issue of postage stamps did not include a six-cent denomination and most people used two three-cent stamps to make up the rate. In rare instances, such as this cover from San Francisco to Boston, a twelve-cent stamp was cut in half and used to pay the six-cent rate. (R. Meyersburg collection)

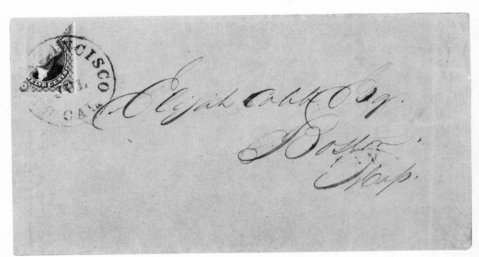

VII The Carrier Stamps

THE STAMPS DISCUSSED IN THE PREVIOUS CHAPTER REPRESENT POS-tage charges for mail transported from one post office to another, or in the case of drop mail, for letters deposited at the same post office where they were to be picked up. But once the mail had reached the office of its destination, it had to be picked up by the recipient at the post office. Some individual post offices of the era, however, did offer pickup or delivery of mail at homes or offices—and this was called "carrier service."

The charge for this carrier service was one cent in addition to the regular charge, prepaid. By the year 1851, we find that a number of post offices which offered such service had issued their own one-cent "carrier stamps" to indicate the payment of that charge. The United States Despatch Post mentioned in chapter 3, for instance, was one of the offices issuing these "semiofficial" stamps.

In 1851, shortly after the new federal issue had been distributed, Nathan Hall in Washington decided to issue a one-cent federal carrier stamp for use by those post offices which wanted to offer carrier service. Of course, the new one-cent stamp of 1851 could have been used for that purpose, but Hall wanted a separate stamp to avoid confusion and to indicate the distinction between *postage* fees and *carrier* fees. Accordingly, he instructed the regular stamp contractor, Toppan, Carpenter, and Casilear, to prepare a one-cent carrier stamp.

The one-cent federal carrier stamp of 1851 featured in the central medallion a portrait of Benjamin Franklin, quite similar to the one on the one-cent postage stamp, except that the portrait on the carrier stamp faced left instead of right. At the top of the carrier stamp was a label with the word

The similarity of design between the one-cent postage stamp of 1851 and the Franklin carrier stamp of the same year is readily apparent in this nose-to-nose comparison. (R. Meyersburg collection)

OPPOSITE: *Carrier stamps are generally found on local or domestic covers, so this black-banded mourning cover bound to Canada is a great rarity. The one-cent eagle carrier stamp paid for service to the mails and the single one-cent and three three-cent postage stamps paid the rate from Philadelphia to Toronto, Canada West. The eagle carrier stamp is tied to the cover by a light stroke of a United States-Canada exchange marking which was applied at the border. (R. Meyersburg collection)*

"CARRIERS" placed between stars enclosed in brackets and at the bottom was the inscription "STAMP" between similar ornaments. The geometric lathework ornaments surrounding the central portrait were derived from the same stock dies used on the three-cent and twelve-cent postage stamps.

Because the stamp contractor was located in Philadelphia, one of the first post office employees to see the new carrier stamp was John C. Montgomery, the assistant postmaster of that city. Knowing that the carrier service was intended to be distinct from the regular mails, Montgomery was dismayed by the great similarity between the designs of the one-cent postage stamp and the new carrier stamp. It was clear that the new stamp was likely to cause problems, and Montgomery decided to advise Hall of the difficulties and to suggest a possible solution. He wrote in a letter of September 27, 1851:

Messrs. Toppan, Carpenter & Co informed me yesterday that they have now ready for delivery a million and a half of the new carriers' stamps, and that they are awaiting a requisition from the P.O. Department. This new stamp is so like the one cent stamp, that I am persuaded it will create great confusion. I had a long conversation with the engravers upon the subject, and they coincided with me in the opinion that some device more easily distinguishable from the Post Office stamps should be adopted, and they offer to furnish a new plate for the purpose without any additional charge to the Department—in the course of a few days they will have completed a design which I will forward to you—they propose to have an oval something like the one I send herewith, with a beautifully executed Eagle in the centre, and around the edge "U.S.P.O. DESPATCH— PREPAID ONE CENT" — this, would designate at once the character of the

Prior to the Franklin and Eagle carrier stamp issue of 1851, several postmasters had produced, with the blessing of the Post Office Department, carrier stamps for use at their own offices. These stamps were only recognized at the local office, but that is all that was necessary because the carrier services were local in nature. The New York post office, after the City Despatch Post was sold back to private ownership, produced a very simple carrier stamp which has come to be known as the lifesaver, because of its shape. This cover bears a copy of the New York carrier stamp (black-on-yellow paper), which paid for carrier service to the mails, and a single five-cent stamp of the 1847 issue, which paid the letter postage rate for less than 300 miles. (R. Meyersburg collection)

stamp, and prevent the possibility of any mistake, and besides, the American Eagle handsomely and artistically executed, would commend itself to the favor of the American People, and would designate at once the nature of the service to which it is to be appropriated, and shew its Post-Official connexion—which the other fails to do—neither the P. Office nor one cent prepaid being lettered on them.

Hall received the letter from Montgomery on September 29 and added the notation, "Thinks Carrier Stamp by Toppan Carpenter & Co too much

The carrier service of the 1840s and 1850s was, for accounting purposes, kept quite separate from the regular postal service. Although postage stamps were often used to pay for carrier service, the stamps produced specifically for that service were not valid for postage, and were rarely accepted at the post office in payment of postal charges. This cover is a rare example of a New York carrier stamp that was accepted for payment of postage. That the three black-on-yellow stamps were indeed accepted is indicated by the "NEW YORK PAID 3Cts." marking, handstamped at the right. There is only one other recorded example of a New York carrier stamp having been used in this manner. (R. Meyersburg collection)

like the one cent letter stamp. Recommends another design."

Montgomery's second letter to the postmaster general was sent on October 5:

> *I have the pleasure of transmitting to you herewith an impression of the beautiful stamp respecting which I wrote to you a few days since. I have exhibited it to a hundred judicious friends, by all of whom it is highly commended. Messrs. Toppan & Co are so much pleased with it, that they*

*In Philadelphia the post office had a handstamp made which read "*U.S.P.O. DISPATCH PRE-PAID ONE CENT." *This was used to cancel postage stamps on letters handled by the carrier service, and to produce carrier stamps by using the gummed paper from the margins of postage-stamp sheets. When the carrier fee on a letter was paid in cash, the handstamp was struck on the face of the cover and canceled with a red crayon. This cover from Bloomfield, New Jersey, was sent to Philadelphia. The addressee was no longer at the original address, and the letter was forwarded to the proper address by way of the carrier service. (R. Meyersburg collection)*

offer to execute the plate and prepare the stamps without any additional charge to the Department—and I trust that it will meet with your approbation, and that you will, at your earliest convenience, give an order for the preparation of the new plate, as it is so far superior to the head of Franklin, this speaking plainly for itself and designating its object—whereas the other will be continually confounded with the one cent stamp of the P.O. Dept., the only difference in the design of the two being, that in the one case, Franklin is looking West, and in the other his face is turned toward the East.

This new stamp tells its own story, and the Eagle will appeal at once to the affections and patriotism of the American People. When I suggested the idea to Mr. Toppan he caught it up avidly, and when he had executed the drawing, he agreed with me that the idea was conceived in "a fit of enthusiasm". I was mistaken, or rather Mr. Toppan was mistaken, in the information he gave me respecting the number of carriers' stamps already printed—he thought the number was 1,500,000, but he informed me yesterday that only 300,000 had been printed—and you would do me a kindness by giving me an order for some thousands of these which would answer our purpose until the new U.S.P.O. Despatch stamp shall have been printed.

Hall was quick to see a good deal when it was placed before him. To be provided with a very handsome stamp which would eliminate the possible confusion that the Franklin design could cause, and without any additional expense to the department, was more than a good deal, it was a windfall. Hall's notation, on the back of Montgomery's second letter, was short and to the point: "October 10, 1851—Design approved and stamps ordered."

The Eagle carrier stamp, the second and final stamp of its type to be

One of the more elaborate designs among the small group of local-official carrier stamps was the stamp produced for use in Baltimore, Maryland. The mounted horseman in the center of the stamp is holding a banner labeled "ONE CENT," and ribbons at the top and bottom are inscribed "GOVERNMENT CITY DISPATCH." The carrier stamp on this August 1859 cover paid for carrier service to the mails, the three-cent stamp being required for postage from the Baltimore post office to Lancaster, Pennsylvania. The Baltimore carrier stamp is unusual in that it remained in service long after the federally produced Franklin and Eagle stamps were available. (R. Meyersburg collection)

issued by the federal government, came into use on November 17, 1851. The Franklin stamps, which had been in service for only about four weeks, were withdrawn when the Eagles arrived from the printer and the remainders were destroyed.

The use of separate stamps for prepayment of carrier fees continued until the early 1860s when the charge for delivery of letters was absorbed into the regular postal charges. The short history of the two carrier stamps of the 1851 issue is one of the interesting episodes in the story of the U.S. postage stamp.

VIII Registered Mail and the First Perforated Issue

IN MAKING HIS PROCLAMATION ABOUT THE NEW POSTAL REGULA-
tions in 1855, James Campbell mentioned one other feature, something he
could not put into operation immediately because of the rush to issue the
needed ten-cent stamps and convert to obligatory prepayment—registry of
mail. The act of 1855 provided for the official registration of mail for the
first time at a cost of five cents, and Campbell said that "special instructions" about this new service would be issued as soon as possible.

This provision for the registry of mail was part of the post office's long-
time campaign to combat mail theft. It had been a problem stretching back
into the previous century when highway robbery of mail riders, and then
stagecoaches, was a constant danger. The government's efforts to thwart
this problem were decisive and apparently quite effective. By the act of 1792,
the robbery of a mail carrier was made punishable by death; however, that
punishment was modified by the act of 1799, which made the sentence forty
lashes plus imprisonment not exceeding ten years for a first offense, but the
death penalty for a second offense or if the stagecoach driver's life was jeop-
ardized by the use of dangerous weapons during the robbery. That last provision was moot in most cases, because highway robbers usually had to
brandish such weapons in order to force the stagecoach driver to stop.

Oliver Holmes and Peter Rohrbach in *Stagecoach East* relate a number
of those daring mail robberies during the first part of the nineteenth century, notably the celebrated robbery of the Great Eastern mail coach on the
night of March 12, 1818. The stagecoach was proceeding toward Philadelphia when it was held up about two miles south of Havre de Grace, Maryland, by three men who had erected a barrier across the road. Armed with

pistols, the robbers tied up the passengers and rifled the mail pouches—and then fled with some $90,000. Two of the men were captured within a few days, and the other ten days later. They were quickly placed on trial, and two of them were condemned to death, while the third, a young man just twenty years of age, was given a jail sentence of ten years. The execution of the two robbers was carried out on September 10 of that same year, less than six months after the actual crime.

That practice of meting out justice quickly and severely seems to have been effective. Return J. Meigs, Jr., who was postmaster general from 1814 to 1823, boasted in his report of 1819 that "since I have been at the head of this Department not one instance of a violent robbery of the mail has occurred, where the perpetrators have escaped apprehension, conviction, and punishment."

The problem of highway robbery of the mail began to diminish in the 1830s as more and more mail was being transported in the greater security of railroad cars, rather than by stagecoaches along often deserted and lonely roads. But in Meigs's boastful statement there is a carefully placed phrase—*violent robbery*—which indicates one problem that had not been solved either in his time or by the time James Campbell occupied the same office thirty-five years later: internal theft of the mail by post office workers. There was a serious temptation for postal workers because the potential rewards of internal mail theft were so great. It must be remembered that this was an era of less sophisticated banking systems and money-transfer operations, and consequently the mail often contained large amounts of cash or negotiable assets. According to contemporary accounts, it was not unusual during the first half of the nineteenth century for the mail pouches along the major routes to contain between $50,000 and $100,000 in bank notes and other transferable paper. It was not until 1864 that the post office established the money-order system, which eliminated the need for "money" letters in the mail. Up until that time the temptation for postal workers to pilfer the mail was always there—and often it was not resisted.

Some individual local postmasters tried to solve the problem between 1845 and 1851 by keeping a register of letters containing currency, securities, or important papers. This service was offered at no cost and it was not authorized by the Post Office Department; all it served to do was keep track of those important letters as they proceeded through the mail system. We find evidences of this local registry of the mail at such post offices as Philadelphia, Mobile, Detroit, and Cleveland. Sometimes special handstamps were used to mark these letters with the letter "R"; at other times the handwritten notations of "Registered" or "Reg'd" were found. And some of the handstamps contained the actual notation "Money Letter," although it is not known if this blatant announcement of the cash contents of a particular letter either increased or decreased the possibility of its theft.

In 1855 the Post Office Department issued the five-cent stamp mentioned in chapter 6, which would be used on some foreign mail as well as registered letters under the new system. The new registry fee was considered distinct from the postage charges at this time, much in the way that the carrier service was distinct from the regular mail service, and the registry fee could thus be paid in cash if the sender wished. It was not until 1867 that the use of stamps to pay registration became compulsory.

The act of 1855 noted that the registration "shall not render the Post Office Department or its revenues liable for the loss of such letter or package, or the contents thereof." Since there was no indemnification, the registry inaugurated in 1855 was, like that of the local postmasters a few years earlier, basically a tracking system to follow important mail through the system, thereby identifying the people who handled it and possibly frightening them away from pilfering it.

In the report he issued on December 3, 1855, Campbell said that it was still too early to evaluate the success of the new registration plan because it had only been in operation a short time, but he did state that the department was working to eradicate every delay it found in the transportation and delivery of registered letters. However, he concluded that he "found abundant proofs of its usefulness, and also of the necessity of perfecting it by such means as experience may suggest." By 1868 the registry fee had been raised to twenty cents, but it was not until 1898 that the post office established an indemnity for lost or stolen mail, a figure set at that time not to exceed $10,000.

~~~

James Campbell established another Post Office Department innovation in 1855: the appointment of the first stamp agent. Prior to that time, all newly printed stamps had been delivered directly to the Post Office Department in Washington, but Campbell changed that with the appointment of Jessey Johnson as United States stamp agent on May 18, 1855. He had his office in the Jayne Building on Chestnut Street in Philadelphia. With his appoint-

The designs of some values of the 1851 issue were placed very close together on the printing plate, making the introduction of perforations between the individual stamps a difficult process. This problem was extreme in the case of the one-cent and ten-cent denominations. To correct the problem, the printers erased part of the designs from the plate, thus allowing adequate room for the perforations to be run. On this strip of three one-cent stamps the erasures between the stamps may be easily seen. (R. Meyersburg collection)

ment, all stamps would be delivered to him at their place of manufacture, and after he had taken possession of them in the name of the United States government, he would deliver them to Washington. Again, this function seemed to have been prompted by the fear of postal theft of actual stamps. This system was continued until February 1, 1869, when the stamp agent forwarded the new stamps through the Registry Division of the New York Post Office directly to the local postmasters who had placed orders for them.

In 1854 Great Britain, using a process developed by Henry Archer, began to issue its postage stamps with perforations to aid in the separation of the single stamps from the sheet. The energetic James Campbell saw that these

The perforating process was new to America and sometimes the accuracy of perforation placement was not very good. If the perforations were far off the intended position, the person operating the perforating machine often made a second attempt at getting the perforations in the space between the stamps. The three-cent stamp on this cover has wide margins at the bottom and left sides, is perforated inside the top label, and received two rows of perforations along the right side. The stamp is canceled with the scarce station handstamp of Cobham, a small stop on the Virginia Central Railroad. (National Philatelic Collection)

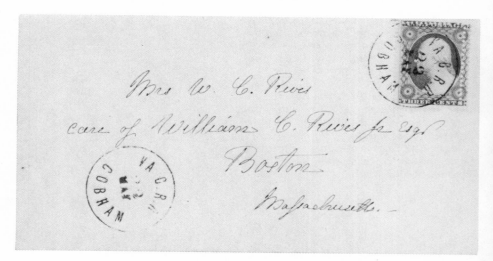

perforations would be of great convenience and he began to study ways in which the process could be duplicated in the production of stamps in the United States. This would be his last major contribution to the United States postal system, culminating in the issue of 1857, which was produced during the last few months of his term as postmaster general.

Franklin Pierce, unpopular in his own party, was not able to obtain renomination at the Democratic convention in 1856, which nominated James Buchanan, who had been secretary of state in Polk's cabinet. Buchanan, in turn, won the national election that year, receiving a considerable amount of help from his old fellow cabinet member Cave Johnson, who helped deliver Tennessee for him. Campbell apparently liked his job as postmaster general and wanted to stay in office, but even though Buchanan was a fellow Democrat, Campbell feared that the incoming President would accept his obligatory resignation and appoint a whole new cabinet. There were, he felt, a few final things he wanted to accomplish while still in office, and late in 1856 he began negotiations with Toppan, Carpenter, and Casilear in Philadelphia for a new issue of postage stamps. He wanted some higher denomination stamps for heavier mail—a twenty-four-cent stamp, a thirty-cent stamp, and a ninety-cent stamp—and, as was being done in England, he wanted them perforated. In fact, he wanted all his stamps to be perforated from that point on, and he instructed the firm to print new stamps in the denominations of the 1851 issue, but with perforations. Campbell needed no authorization from Congress for this issue because the act of 1851 allowed him to issue stamps of "such other denominations as he may think necessary" for delivering the mail. The process of perforation was simply a detail of manufacture in the production of these stamps.

Toppan, Carpenter, and Casilear, however, had some reservations about accepting Campbell's order in early 1857, because their original contract with the government was to expire in a few months and there was no guarantee that it would be renewed. If it were not renewed, the firm would have incurred the large cost of obtaining a perforating machine and engraving new plates for a press run of only a few months. Campbell, of course, could not guarantee his own job in the months ahead, much less the Post Office

Three one-cent stamps paid the postage on this cover from Lawrence, Kansas Territory, to Rochester, New York. (National Philatelic Collection)

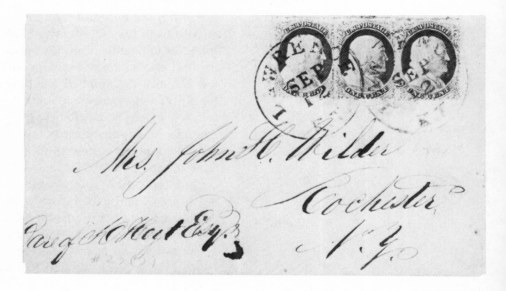

Department's printing contract, but he did listen sympathetically to a Toppan, Carpenter, and Casilear proposal. They asked that, if the contract were not renewed, the government would then indemnify them with the sum of $500 for each engraving the firm had made, plus $3,000 for the perforating machine, all of which would become the property of the government. (The printing contract was, as we noted earlier, indeed renewed, and it ran until after the start of the Civil War in 1861.) Campbell readily agreed, signing

During the 1850s, the use of envelopes as an advertising medium grew rapidly. Many companies produced colorful and elaborate designs, an example being this 1858 cover advertising the Charter Oak Life Insurance Company of Hartford, Connecticut. (R. Meyersburg collection)

the contract, and the first stamps of the issue of 1857 were delivered in late February of that year. All of them were perforated, the first of their kind in U.S. postal history.

The perforated sheets of 1857 stamps were produced on a machine purchased from Wm. Bemrose & Sons of Derby, England. The machine was equipped with a set of perforating rollers which could be rolled across the

Steamboats under contract to the post office carried mail in coastal as well as inland waters. This May 1860 cover was carried from Newport, Rhode Island, to Providence by the steamer Perry. *The cover was probably handed on board at the dock in Newport, and thus the three-cent stamp, which paid the postage, was not canceled until the mail was turned over to the post office in Providence. The envelope itself is stationery from Fillmore House, a guest house in Newport. (National Philatelic Collection)*

printed sheets, once horizontally and once vertically, to produce the perforated stamps. The spacing between the rollers could be varied to accommodate stamps of differing lengths or widths, and of course the setting had to be changed between the horizontal run and the vertical run to accommodate the different lengths and widths of individual stamps. Philatelic historian Lester Brookman is of the opinion that there was a limitation on the width of this machine, which would explain why the vertical lines of the stamps on the sheets of the 1857 issue are set so closely together.

Even small railroads were used to carry the government's mail when their routes ran through areas that were in need of service. On some rail routes the individual stations had their own handstamp devices for canceling mail. This cover bears a complete strike of the very rare marking from Spring Station, a small stop on the Louisville & Frankfort & Lexington & Frankfort Rail Road, an obscure line in the central Kentucky region. The cover was mailed on January 18, 1861, and was received in Lexington the next day. (National Philatelic Collection)

The eight stamps of the 1857 issue were:

One cent. This stamp, as well as the other stamps of the 1851 denominations, are the same as the original issue, although sometimes slight alterations were made on the edges of the design in order to accommodate the perforations.

Three cents. Same as 1851, but the horizontal frame lines at the top and bottom were removed.

Five cents. Same as the 1851 issue, except that the outer line of color on

The rates for international mails were quite complicated, often leading to letters being over- or underpaid. This confusion was not confined to members of the public, but extended also to the postmasters of small towns who rarely had to process letters to foreign destinations. Sometimes the mistakes in rating of foreign mail even slipped past the foreign-mail clerks in large offices such as New York. This cover, posted at Loch Lomond, Virginia, on April 14, 1860, was destined for France and, since the letter weighed more than ¼ ounce but less than ½ ounce, it should have been rated at thirty-cents—twice the single rate of fifteen cents. For some reason, the postmaster at Loch Lomond received only twenty-four cents in postage (seven three-cent stamps and a three-cent stamped envelope), and sent the letter on to New York for the next mail packet for France. At New York the foreign-division clerk missed the error and struck the cover with a handstamp crediting France with twenty-four cents, the entire amount of postage collected. The French accepted the New York marking at face value and did not charge additional postage on the letter, as evidenced by the boxed "P.D." marking. Thus, the United States gave the entire twenty-four cents it had collected on this

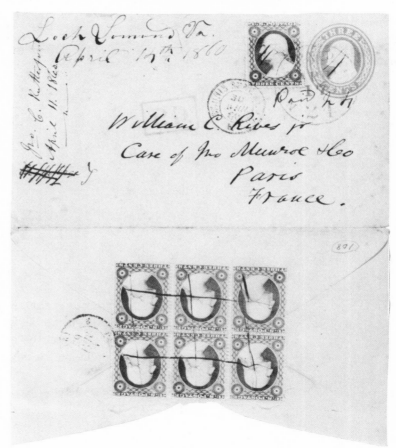

This cover represents correct payment of the fifteen-cent rate to France—use of a five-cent and a ten-cent stamp being a common combination. The cover was sent by direct service to Le Havre, France, from New York, resulting in a credit of only three cents to France. (R. Meyersburg collection)

cover to the French, keeping nothing for itself. Problems such as this were what the uniform ocean postage advocates wished to avoid. (National Philatelic Collection)

the projecting ornaments at top and bottom were cut away, which is usually described as "ornaments partly removed."

Ten cents. Same as 1851.

Twelve cents. Same as 1851.

Twenty-four cents. A new stamp featuring a portrait of George Washington by Stuart on an oval disk surrounded by a solid, curved border. Although the plates for this stamp were made in 1857, the stamp was not put

An exceptionally fine copy of the ten-cent stamp of 1857 graces this cover from Keene, New Hampshire, to Dundus, Canada West, mailed on December 23, 1859. (R. Meyersburg collection)

OPPOSITE: *The steam-powered ships of the late 1850s and 1860s were able to cross the Atlantic in only twelve days. The cover bearing a pair of the twelve-cent stamps of the 1857 issue was probably carried on a vessel which looked very much like the packet boat shown on the illustrated envelope. The cover was carried from New York to Liverpool by an American packet in late July 1860. The British post office received three cents for inland postage, and the remaining twenty-one cents were retained by the U.S. post office as payment for inland postage (five cents) and sea postage (sixteen cents). (R. Meyersburg collection)*

into actual use until 1860. Color, very dark lilac.

Thirty cents. A profile bust of Benjamin Franklin on an oval disk with a slightly shaded border. In each of the four corners is a shield, placed obliquely, with fine radiations, connected with ornate, shaded scrolls. Color, orange. Again, although this plate was made in 1857, the stamp was not put into use until 1860.

Ninety cents. A portrait of George Washington in the dress uniform of a

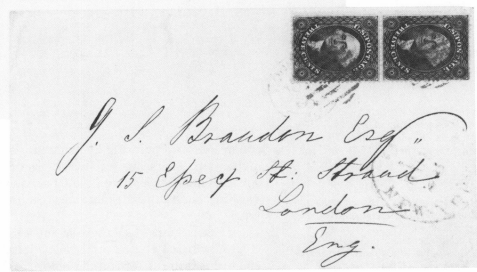

The three high values of the 1857 issue
were finally released in 1860, and it was
then possible to pay the postage on a single
letter to England by affixing a single
postage stamp. This May 1861 cover from
New York to Torrington, England, was
carried by British packet, resulting in a
credit of nineteen cents to Britain for sea
postage and inland postage. The twenty-
four-cent stamps were printed quite close to
one another and copies such as this one,
which show the entire design, are not
common. (R. Meyersburg collection)

OPPOSITE: The higher denominations of the
1857 issue are not common on covers
because they were in service for only a year
before being demonetized at the beginning
of the Civil War. This small cover, franked
with both a three-cent and thirty-cent
postage stamp, was sent from Yonkers, New
York, to Manila in the Philippines. The
cover was mailed on April 1, 1861, and left
New York April 3 on board the Cunard
Line ship Canada, bound for Liverpool,
England. From Liverpool, the cover
traveled to London and was placed on the
next available ship bound for Hong Kong,
arriving there on June 6. It is unclear how
the cover was transported from Hong Kong
to Manila, although a likely possibility is
that a representative of Russell and

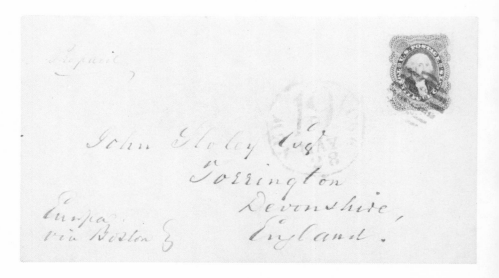

general, after a painting by Trumbull, on a very dark oblong ground with
arched top. There are scrollwork ornaments. Brookman calls this "one of
our most handsome stamps," and he says that it does "real justice" to George
Washington. Again, the plate was made in 1857, but the stamp was not used
until 1860.

These stamps, like those of the 1851 issue, are found in a number of
"types," which is beyond our scope, but there is one interesting thing to note
about this issue of 1857: it did not invalidate the issue of 1851, as the issue

Company, a Hong Kong forwarding agent, carried the letter in a company pouch to Manila, and delivered it to Russell and Sturgis, an affiliated company to whose care the letter is addressed. At any rate, the addressee's docketing mark on the back of the envelope indicates that the letter reached him on June 11, 1861. Of the total postage of thirty-three cents, the United States kept only five cents, the remaining twenty-eight cents being credited to Britain for sea postage (sixteen cents) and colonial transit (twelve cents). (National Philatelic Collection)

of 1851 had invalidated the issue of 1847. Those stamps of 1851 were still valid whenever they could be found, and thus all the stamps of 1851–57 continued to be valid until 1861 when, as we shall see, the Union demonetized all existing stamps. But by the year 1860, the last full year of the 1857 issue, the post office was issuing more than 216,000,000 of these stamps annually.

In late 1860 the postmaster general issued an order requiring that postage stamps be obliterated with a handstamp other than the town's name handstamp. More than a year earlier, Marcus Norton of Troy, New York, had applied for and been granted a patent for a stamp-canceling device which incorporated both a circular date stamp with the town's name and grid for obliterating the postage stamp. Not knowing of Norton's patent, the post office at New York developed a similar device for use in accordance with the postmaster general's orders. This new device was an infringement on Norton's patent, and in an attempt to correct the problem, and at the same time secure a contract for the production of post office handstamps, Norton offered to let the New York office use his handstamps for a short time without any compensation. The post office soon decided that, patent or no patent, it was easier to make the handstamps themselves, and discontinued use of the Norton product. This style of "duplex" marking soon became standard throughout the country, and litigation on behalf of Norton's heirs and assigns continues to this day. These two covers show use of the Norton Patent handstamp and the New York copy on the same date, February 9, 1861. (National Philatelic Collection)

IX Westward Ho for the Stamp

JAMES CAMPBELL'S POLITICAL INSTINCTS WERE CORRECT, AND THE incoming President Buchanan accepted his resignation, sending the "fat and jolly" Irishman back to Philadelphia where he practiced law the remainder of his life. In his place, Buchanan in 1857 appointed Aaron V. Brown, a former congressman and governor of Tennessee, who was to have a relatively brief tenure as postmaster general because he died two years after his appointment. However, the sixty-two-year-old lawyer-politician made some significant contributions during his term, particularly in establishing the overland mail routes to the West Coast.

During the fifteen years immediately prior to the outbreak of the Civil War, the postal service had been developing significantly in the West and Southwest. In Texas, for instance, there were 119 post offices in 1846, but that number had increased to 923 post offices by the start of the Civil War in 1861. And mail service was being established elsewhere west of the Mississippi during those years. The Mormon settlement in Utah was served by private mail carriers as early as 1847. Federal post offices were established in Oregon City in 1847, at San Francisco in 1848, and Salt Lake City in 1849. During those years the United States military provided courier service between its posts, and at times this service was made available to the public. Kit Carson, while employed by the army, carried the first overland mail from coast-to-coast in 1848.

By the time Aaron Brown became postmaster general in 1857, there were some transcontinental overland mail routes, often painfully slow, but until he took office the most significant and successful coast-to-coast mail service was actually made mostly on water. After the discovery of gold in

A Concord coach, loaded with passengers and mail, heads west at a rapid pace in this period woodcut. (From the Library of Congress)

California on January 24, 1848, migration to the West increased dramatically as fortune-seekers headed for Sutter's Mill near Sacramento. In that same year the Post Office Department awarded a contract to a firm, which became known as the Pacific Mail Steamship Company, to carry transcontinental mail over an "ocean route." Under this contract, the mail traveled by ship from New York to Panama, was transported on land across the Isthmus of Panama, and then again by ship to San Francisco and Oregon. In 1855 the transit across the isthmus was improved by the completion of the Panama railroad, and by 1858 the scheduled time for transporting mail between New York and San Francisco was between three and four weeks, although in practice it often took longer than that.

There had been agitation in Congress for some time to develop an overland transcontinental mail route, thus eliminating the tortuous trip down to Panama and up the coast. Accordingly, on March 3, 1857, Congress passed legislation authorizing a mail route between such "a point on the Mississippi river as the contractors may select" and San Francisco. It was the task of the new postmaster general, Aaron Brown, to implement this act, and the way he did it caused some furor and cries of scandal in Washington.

Despite the stipulations of the act, Brown selected a route that began with *two* roads, one starting at Memphis, Tennessee, and the other at St. Louis, Missouri. The route converged at Little Rock, Arkansas, and proceeded to Preston, Texas, and then on to Fort Yuma and San Francisco. This route—which became known as the "Southern Route"—was sharply criticized by northern congressmen, who said that the act had mentioned nothing about the link from Tennessee. Aaron Brown was, of course, from Tennessee.

Nevertheless, Brown stuck to his plan, and roads along the route were improved under the direction of the secretary of the interior. Brown awarded the contract for actually carrying the mail to the Overland Mail Company, a stagecoach firm owned by John Butterfield, who began service on the route on September 15, 1858. Butterfield used the famed Concord coaches, which

No. 1.] **[Sep. 16th, 1858.**

OVERLAND MAIL COMPANY.

THROUGH TIME SCHEDULE BETWEEN

ST. LOUIS, MO., MEMPHIS, TENN. } & SAN FRANCISCO, CAL.

GOING WEST. GOING EAST.

LEAVE.	DAYS.	Hour.	Distance, Place to Place.	Time allowed.	Av'ge Miles per Hour.	LEAVE.	DAYS.	Hour.	Distance, Place to Place.	Time allowed.	Av'ge Miles per Hour.
St. Louis, Mo., & Memphis, Tenn. }	Every Monday & Thursday,	8.00 A.M	Miles.	No. Hours		San Francisco, Cal.	Every Monday & Thursday,	8.00 A.M	Miles.	No. Hours	
P. R. R. Terminus, "	" Monday & Thursday,	6.00 P.M	160	10	16	Firebaugh's Ferry, "	" Tuesday & Friday,	11.00 A.M	163	27	6
Springfield, "	" Wednesday & Saturday	7.45 A.M	143	37¾	3 7/9	Visalia, "	" Wednesday & Saturday,	5.00 A.M	82	18	4½
Fayetteville, "	" Thursday & Sunday,	10.15 A.M	100	26½	3 7/9	Ft. Tejon, (Via Los Angeles to)	" Thursday & Sunday,	9.00 A.M	127	28	4½
Fort Smith, Ark.	" Friday & Monday,	3.30 A.M	65	17¼	3 7/9	San Bernardino, "	" Friday & Monday,	5.30 P.M	150	32½	4½
Sherman, Texas	" Sunday & Wednesday,	12.30 A.M	205	45	4½	Fort Yuma, "	" Sunday & Wednesday,	1.30 P.M	200	44	4½
Fort Belknap. "	" Monday & Thursday,	9.00 A.M	146½	32½	4½	Gila River,* Arizona	" Monday & Thursday,	7.30 P.M	135	30	4½
Fort Chadbourn, "	" Tuesday & Friday,	3.15 P.M	136	30¼	4½	Tucson, "	" Wednesday & Saturday	3.00 A.M	141	31½	4½
Pecos River, (Em. Crossing.)	" Thursday & Sunday,	3.45 A.M	165	36½	4½	Soldier's Farewell,	" Thursday & Sunday,	8.00 P.M	184½	41	4½
El Paso,	" Saturday & Tuesday,	11.00 A.M	248½	55¼	4½	El Paso, Tex.	" Saturday & Tuesday,	5.30 A.M	150	33½	4½
Soldier's Farewell	" Sunday & Wednesday,	8.30 P.M	150	33½	4½	Pecos River, (Em. Crossing)	" Monday & Thursday	12.45 P.M	248½	55¼	4½
Tucson, Arizona	" Tuesday & Friday,	1.30 P.M	184½	41	4½	Fort Chadbourn, "	" Wednesday & Saturday	1.15 A.M	165	36½	4½
Gila River,* "	" Wednesday & Saturday	9.00 P.M	141	31½	4½	Fort Belknap, "	" Thursday & Sunday,	7.30 A.M	136	30¼	4½
Fort Yuma, Cal.	" Friday & Monday,	3.00 A.M	135	30	4½	Sherman, "	" Friday & Monday,	4.00 P.M	146½	32½	4½
San Bernardino "	" Saturday & Tuesday,	11.00 P.M	200	44	4½	Fort Smith, Ark.	" Sunday & Wednesday,	1.00 P.M	205	45	4½
Ft. Tejon, (Via Los Angeles.)	" Monday & Thursday,	7.30 A.M	150	32½	4½	Fayetteville, Mo.	" Monday, & Thursday,	6.15 A.M	65	17¼	3 7/9
Visalia, "	" Tuesday & Friday,	11.30 A.M	127	28	4½	Springfield, "	" Tuesday & Friday,	8.45 A.M	100	26½	3 7/9
Firebaugh's Ferry, "	" Wednesday & Saturday	5.30 A.M	82	18	4½	P. R. R. Terminus, "	" Wednesday & Saturday	10.30 P.M	143	37¾	3 7/9
(Arrive) San Francisco,	" Thursday & Sunday,	8.30 A.M	163	27	6	(Arrive) St. Louis, Mo., & Memphis, Tenn. }	" Thursday & Sunday,		160	10	16

This Schedule may not be exact—Superintendents, Agents, Station-men, Conductors, Drivers and all employees are particularly directed to use every possible exertion to get the Stages through in quick time, even though they may be ahead of this time.

If they are behind this time, it will be necessary to urge the animals on to the highest speed that they can be driven without injury.

Remember that no allowance is made in the time for ferries, changing teams, &c. It is therefore necessary that each driver increase his speed over the average per hour enough to gain the necessary time for meals, changing teams, crossing ferries, &c.

Every person in the Company's employ will always bear in mind that each minute of time is of importance. If each driver on the route loses fifteen (15) minutes, it would make a total loss of time, on the entire route, of twenty-five (25) hours, or, more than one day. If each one loses ten (10) minutes it would make a total loss of sixteen and one half (16½) hours, or, the best part of a day.

On the contrary, if each driver gains that amount of time, it leaves a margin of time against accidents and extra delays.

All hands will see the great necessity of promptness and dispatch: every minute of time is valuable as the Company are under heavy forfeit if the mail is behind time.

Conductors must note the hour and date of departure from Stations, the causes of delay, if any, and all particulars. They must also report the same fully to their respective Superintendents.

* The Station referred to on Gila River, is 40 miles west of Maricopa Wells.

JOHN BUTTERFIELD.
Pres't.

were manufactured in Concord, New Hampshire, and which could carry five to six hundred pounds of mail, as well as four passengers and their baggage. The initial trips from St. Louis to San Francisco were completed ahead of their scheduled twenty-five days, and that time was improved over the years as more relay stations were set up along the route, allowing the teams of horses to be changed every ten or fifteen miles. Butterfield's initial contract gave him $600,000 annually for semiweekly mail service along that route.

But the success of this Southern Route did not diminish the outrage of those congressmen who held northern interests, and they continued to pressure for a change. Brown, on the other hand, devoted seventeen pages of fine print in his annual report for 1858 to justify his selection of the route and to answer his critics. To his credit, though, Brown continued to improve other western routes, and he especially attempted to show no partiality to either the North or the South during those two critical years when the nation was on the verge of coming asunder. After his death, and after a new administration was on its way into Washington, Brown's critics finally were victorious, when Congress passed the act of March 2, 1861, just weeks before the beginning of the Civil War. This act provided for a new transcontinental mail route. Called the "Central Route," it carried the mails over a more northerly course, starting in St. Joseph, Missouri, and passing through Denver and Salt Lake City and then on to San Francisco. The contract was again given to John Butterfield, who switched his mail service to the Central Route on July 1, 1861. But by that time, of course, more serious and savage concerns occupied the young Republic.

After Aaron Brown died in March 1859, President Buchanan appointed Joseph Holt, a sixty-five-year-old Kentucky lawyer, as postmaster general. Holt was an anomaly among postmasters general in that he had never held an elective political office. He was an extremely successful lawyer in Louisville and also in Mississippi, and he had a wide reputation as an outstanding orator. (Incidentally, he had married Margaret Wickliffe, the daughter of Charles "Duke" Wickliffe, whom we met earlier as Tyler's postmaster general.) In the national election of 1856, Holt used his famed oratorical skills widely in speaking for the Democratic party and the election of James Buchanan, and after Buchanan was elected, he invited him to come to Washington in 1857 as commissioner of patents, an act of political gratitude as eternal as politics itself. Now, in 1859, the President appointed the Duke's son-in-law postmaster general, another step up for this Washington newcomer who was to become a major and controversial figure in the city during the coming war and especially in its aftermath.

During Holt's term as postmaster general there began one of the most romantic and dramatic episodes in the whole history of the American postal system—the famed "Pony Express." This western pony express, however, was not originally established by the post office, but was the work of William H. Russell, an American transportation pioneer.

Russell was the chief partner in the firm of Russell, Majors & Waddell, which operated a stagecoach line with the elongated name of the Central Overland, California & Pike's Peak Express Company. Their stages ran along portions of the route to the West Coast which would later be called the Central Route. In 1860 Russell had the idea of establishing an express mail line

THE OVERLAND MAIL—CHANGING STAGE-COACH FOR CELERITY WAGON.

along this route which would be considerably faster than the Butterfield stagecoaches, which were running along the Southern Route. And to deliver his express mail, Russell proposed to pack it in pouches carried by experienced riders on fast horses—it would be a *Pony* Express.

However, Joseph Holt in Washington was cool toward the idea, just as his father-in-law had been cool to the idea of postage stamps twenty-nine years earlier. The debate was still raging in Congress over the Southern Route, which his Tennessee predecessor had established, and Holt did not want to add any more fuel to the fire by establishing what would be in effect a U.S. Central Mail Route operating in competition with the contract Southern Route. Receiving no encouragement in Washington, Russell decided that his firm would go it alone and operate the Pony Express as a private mail service. He started to organize it in the early spring of 1860, much in the way Greig's Post issued the first postage stamp in 1842 when the federal government had no interest in doing so. History repeats itself.

Russell first searched for good horseflesh, fast animals hardy enough to challenge deserts and mountains, and to withstand thirst in the summer and ice in the winter. These horses were dispersed at some 120 relay stations along the Central Route, and during the two-year history of the Pony Express some five hundred horses would be used. Riders were also recruited, and Russell was looking for small, experienced riders. In March 1860 he placed this advertisement in newspapers around the country:

Wanted: Young, skinny, wiry fellows not over 18. Must be expert riders willing to risk death daily. Orphans preferred.

Russell was eventually to recruit some ninety riders, and before being hired, they had to swear on a Bible not to cuss, fight, or abuse their animals, and to conduct themselves honestly. Some of those Pony Express riders of 1860–61 were to become legends in their own time.

The saddles to be used were extremely light in weight and were covered by a saddle cover called a *mochilla*—a rectangular sheet of leather with four pouches for carrying the mail and with cut-outs for the saddle horn and seat. When the rider changed mounts at a relay station, he pulled the *mochilla* quickly from the first horse and threw it over the saddle of the second horse, thereby eliminating the time which otherwise would be needed to transfer the mail from the saddle pouch of the first horse to the pouch of the new horse.

There was some skepticism at the time that Russell would be able to operate such a Pony Express as he planned. St. Joseph, Missouri, the starting place, was a good strategic point for beginning the direct 1,966-mile ride to the West Coast, but the route beyond St. Joseph was often a vast, silent wilderness, inhabited primarily by frequently hostile Indians. Furthermore, there were the extreme weather conditions the riders and horses would encounter: fierce heat in the summer and frigid cold in the winter. But Russell was undaunted. He figured that his riders could make some seventy-five to one hundred miles a day, changing horses regularly at relay stations set about ten or fifteen miles apart. He also estimated that the total time spent at a relay station where the rider whisked the *mochilla* from one horse to another would be two minutes. And as for the Indians? Why, his "boys" would simply outride them on their fast horses.

On April 3, 1860, the Pony Express was launched. The rider that day was Billy Richardson, and he departed St. Joseph with the mail for San Francisco at 6:30 a.m. Billy arrived at Salt Lake City exactly six days later, changing mounts along the way; he passed through Carson City, Nevada, at 2:30 a.m. on April 12, and finally arrived at Sacramento, California, at 5:30 p.m. on the 13th. Horse and rider boarded the steamboat at Sacramento and reached San Francisco at 1:30 a.m. on April 14, to a reception of cheers, band music, and speeches. Billy Richardson was a hero!

The first 2,000-mile trip had been completed in ten and one-half days, which was exactly Russell's schedule. It was less than half the time the stages were taking along the Southern Route, which fueled additional controversy in Congress about altering the route. Russell's Pony Express was an operational success, therefore, and the young riders became familiar figures as they galloped madly along open roads during those two years. Mark Twain, who described a trip west from Missouri to Nevada in *Roughing It*, wrote about the Pony Express rider in these vivid terms:

> *Here he comes! Away across the endless dead level of the prairie a black speck appears against the sky. . . . In a second or two it becomes a horse and rider, rising and falling, rising and falling,—sweeping toward us nearer and nearer—growing more and more distinct, more and more sharply defined . . . and the flutter of hoofs comes faintly to the ear— another instant a whoop and a hurrah from our upper deck, a wave of the rider's hand, but no reply, and man and horse burst past our excited faces, and go swinging away like a belated fragment of a storm!*

The drama of the Pony Express is clearly shown in Changing Horses, *a print by the famous American artist Frederic Remington. (National Philatelic Collection)*

Letters on the Pony Express were first carried over the whole route at the rate of $5.00 per half ounce, but in April of the following year (1861) that fee was reduced to $2.00 per half ounce. The fee was further reduced to

$1.00 per half ounce on July 1, but that was when the Central Route had become the official post office route. Letters were often written on tissue to conserve weight and to stay within the one-half-ounce rate, and during its brief history, the Pony Express carried a considerable number of these letters. Records show that between November 1860 and April 1861 an average of forty-one letters were carried on each westward trip. By July that average had increased to sixty-four letters, and by October of that year, when the Express was terminated, an average of ninety letters were being carried by each rider. Eastbound mails were significantly heavier, with 205 letters carried on one of the first eastbound trips, and by the end of the Pony Express service, the eastbound run averaged about 350 letters a rider.

One of the most remarkable Pony Express rides in the service's short and colorful history was made in March 1861 to carry Lincoln's First Inaugural Address to California. Because of the importance of keeping that state in the Union, as the Civil War was about to break out, it was considered vital to get that historic and eloquent address out there immediately. Lincoln spoke of secession as the "essence of anarchy," and pleaded that "we must not be enemies," asking that all differences be settled "by the better angels of our nature." Elaborate plans were made to speed the speech from St. Joseph to Sacramento, which entailed not only changing horses at relay stops but also changing riders occasionally.

One of the most dangerous stretches of that long run was the 120 miles from Smith's Creek, Nevada, to Fort Churchill, which was particularly hazardous because of the warring Paiutes. "Pony Bob" Haslam was selected to make the run over those dangerous trails, and he was waiting by his horse when the copy of Lincoln's speech arrived in Smith's Creek. He slapped the *mochilla* from the arriving mount over his horse, and galloped off toward Cold Spring, Nevada, making the fastest run ever between Smith's Creek and Cold Spring. Pony Bob changed horses there, and he asked for "Old Buck" as his mount, a familiar horse which he had used before to outrun Indians.

He took off again, but in the middle of the run he encountered an ambush, being first warned of it by Old Buck himself, who pointed his ears forward and snorted just before the Indians charged out of the brush, firing bullets and arrows at him. Pony Bob cocked his gun and urged Old Buck on, hoping to outrun the Indian ponies as he had done in the past. Only this time there was something quite different: the Indians were riding on Pony Express mounts which they had stolen during a raid on a relay station, and Pony Bob could not outride those swift mounts. Wheeling around, he started shooting at the ponies, knocking them out from under the Indians. An arrow struck him in the left arm and remained there quivering while Pony Bob continued to fire. After slowing the Indian charge, he dashed off again, pulling the arrow from his arm, but there were still three Indians coming after him in single file, and methodically he picked two of them off with his pistol. Tossing away that now empty pistol, he drew the other one to dispatch the final Indian, but an arrow tore into his cheek, knocking out five teeth and fracturing his jaw. He continued to fire until his gun was empty, and when he looked around the final Indian was gone.

Injured and hurting, Pony Bob continued on to the next relay station at Middle Gate, slumped over Old Buck but still riding at full speed. At

Middle Gate the station keepers wanted to change riders, but Pony Bob refused: he had contracted to ride to Fort Churchill, and that was what he intended to do. He mounted a horse, and although badly wounded, raced on to Fort Churchill, completing the entire 120 mile run in eight hours and ten minutes. Pony Bob Haslam is part of the legend and the lore of the Pony Express.

William Russell's Pony Express was a success in every aspect but one: he was able to deliver the mail on time, but he was not able to do it at a profit to his firm. The total receipts for the entire Pony Express operation amounted to only $91,404, and Russell's firm lost an estimated half million dollars on the enterprise. The Pony Express was operated as a private enterprise until July 1, 1861, when it went under contract to the U.S. Post Office as an official mail route. On October 26, 1861, the transcontinental telegraph was completed with the meeting of the two lines at Salt Lake City, and the Pony Express came to an end. The Pony Express had operated for only about nineteen months, but it was a uniquely romantic and colorful chapter in the nation's history.

The year 1860 marked the end of an era for the postage stamp and mail delivery in America. During 1861 the Civil War would cause a split in the well-developed postal services in America, spawning new stamp issues to serve both North and South. But the fifteen years prior to the war had been ones of enormous growth, culminating in a mail system which was truly

U.S. Postal Service, 1845–1860

Year Ending June 30	Number of Post Offices	Revenue	Expenditures	Postage Stamps Issued	Stamped Envelopes and Wrappers Issued
1845	14,183	$4,289,842	$4,320,732	None	None
1850	18,417	5,499,985	5,212,953	1,540,545	None
1855	24,410	6,642,136	9,968,342	72,977,300	23,451,725
1860	28,498	8,518,067	14,874,601	216,370,660	29,280,025

transcontinental. The above table indicates just how impressive that growth had been. It shows that the issuance of stamps had increased dramatically in 1855, when their use became compulsory, but during the next five years the number of stamps issued almost tripled in number. Another interesting, and perhaps ironic fact to note is that when stamps became compulsory, the deficit for the Post Office Department began to escalate severely. In 1845 there was only a small deficit, and by 1850 the post office was actually showing a profit. Then in 1855 there was a deficit of more than three million dollars, and by 1860 a deficit of more than six million. Those deficits continued throughout the entire next decade—except for the year of 1865, the last year of the war, when the Union Post Office Department showed a profit of almost a million dollars—but the deficits of the 1860s were not as severe as the earlier ones.

The situation in the United States, therefore, was quite different from that in Britain, where the government was having difficulty in equalling the original postal revenues prior to reform. But at the same time the British were narrowing the margin between deficit and surplus, and in the early 1860s they would begin to show a regular surplus. In America, on the other hand, there was no difficulty in reaching those original gross revenues, but after postal reform the expenditures began to rise dramatically. Of course the postal system in America, where new frontiers were being opened in a vast country and mail often had to be transported huge distances over often primitive territory, was quite different. (William Russell had, in fact, demonstrated just how expensive it was to offer express transcontinental mail, and after the Pony Express ceased to operate his company declared bankruptcy and he had to sell its assets to satisfy creditors.)

∽∾

The Democrats in 1860, bitterly and severely divided over the slavery issue, nominated Stephen A. Douglas as their presidential candidate. He was opposed by the Republican antislavery candidate, Abraham Lincoln, a former Whig and prairie lawyer, who ran under the winning sobriquet "Honest Abe." When Lincoln won the election on November 6, fissures quickly began to appear in the national structure, and an article in the *Charleston Mercury* declared immediately after the election that "the revolution of 1860 has been initiated." Then, on December 20, 1860, South Carolina seceded from the Union, soon to be followed by other southern states. The problem was that Lincoln could take no authoritative action at that time because he would not be officially inaugurated until March 4 of the following year. Two days after South Carolina's secession, Lincoln wrote to his old friend, Alexander Stephens of Georgia, who would become the vice president of the Confederacy: "You think slavery is right and ought to be extended; while we think it is wrong and ought to be restricted. That I suppose is the rub."

The real *rub* that winter of 1860–61 in Washington was that James Buchanan was still President, and while he had a laissez-faire attitude about slavery and wanted the individual states to settle the question themselves, he was strongly committed to the preservation of the Union. He also bitterly blamed Lincoln for what was happening, but as President he began to take precautions for the possibility that war might break out during those last few months of his term. Assessing his cabinet members, Buchanan saw that he had some real weak links in that time of crisis. One of them was Secretary of War John Floyd of Virginia, a secessionist under suspicion of treason for having transferred arms to southern arsenals. Buchanan decided to replace him immediately.

In reviewing candidates for that important position, Buchanan's attention was drawn to his postmaster general, Joseph Holt, who during his two years in Washington had become the new breed of postmasters general who used their cabinet position as a pulpit to speak out on and influence other national matters. The eloquent Holt was a staunch Unionist, and in an article in the *Pittsburgh Chronicle* of November 30, 1860, which was widely quoted in Washington, he proclaimed his loyalty to the Union and spoke of "a faint hesitating hope that the North will do justice to the South and save the Republic before the wreck is complete." On January 1, 1861, Buchanan appointed Holt secretary of war.

Holt played a vigorous role in Buchanan's government during its last two months and he involved himself in the Fort Sumter crisis, which was to be the flashpoint of the Civil War, urging Buchanan to adopt a policy of firmness. Joseph Holt left the government with Buchanan in March 1861, of course, but the following year Abraham Lincoln was attracted by this "War Democrat," and although he was of an opposing party he appointed him to the new and quite controversial office of judge-advocate general of the army. In that role, Holt was able to arrest civilians and convict them of disloyal activities in a military court, using procedures which would not have been allowed in a civilian court.

Holt's appointment as secretary of war in 1861 had meant that Buchanan had to find another postmaster general for those few months. He was looking for a strong Unionist, of course, and he found one right in the Post Office Department itself: Horatio King, a twenty-two-year career employee who had served as first-assistant postmaster general during the previous two administrations. In addition, like his superior in the department, this Maine native was an outspoken proponent of the Union and he had even admonished Representative John Ashmore of South Carolina that his state's continued use of the mails was evidence that it was still in the Union, despite the Act of Secession. The most significant thing that happened in the department during King's two-month term as postmaster general was the congressional act of February 27, 1861, which raised to ten cents the rate for all mail transported from east of the Rocky Mountains to the West Coast and vice versa, in an attempt to recoup some of the enormous costs people like William Russell had experienced in those primitive areas. After the war, Horatio King retired from government and started a law practice specializing in war claims, which made him a wealthy man, and in 1895, late in his life, he published a book which was a defense of the Buchanan administration, *Turning on the Light*.

Montgomery Blair, postmaster general appointed by Abraham Lincoln in 1861.

But the lights were going out when Abraham Lincoln was sworn in as the nation's sixteenth President on March 4, 1861. On the following day he was advised by Major Robert Anderson, the commandant at Fort Sumter in South Carolina that he could only hold out for a little while longer if he did not receive supplies. Fort Sumter had become a major symbolic cause for the new Confederacy which had been declared on February 4. It was only a small fort on an island at the entrance of Charleston harbor, but the Confederacy wanted Lincoln to withdraw the Union troops because it did not want a "foreign power" to hold a fort in one of its principal harbors.

At a cabinet meeting on March 15, Secretary of State William Seward led a group which urged Lincoln to evacuate the fort in order to avoid war. There was only one cabinet member who unequivocally urged reinforcement of Fort Sumter: the new postmaster general, Montgomery Blair, who, as we shall see, was to be another politically active postmaster general. Blair argued forcefully for the reinforcement, threatening to resign if the fort was surrendered, and eventually Lincoln came around to Blair's way of thinking, announcing on April 6 that he was sending a supply ship to Fort Sumter.

Pierre Gustave Beauregard, the Confederate commandant at Charleston, then asked Major Anderson to surrender, and when he refused, the Confederate forces opened fire on Fort Sumter on April 12. After thirty-four hours of bombardment, during which large portions of the fort were destroyed, the Union garrison surrendered, even though quite amazingly not a man on either side was killed. But that would change in the years ahead, because on April 14, 1861, the United States flag was pulled down at Fort Sumter, and the bloody fratricidal struggle that was to last four years had begun.

X The Civil War: Issue of 1861

ABRAHAM LINCOLN'S APPOINTEE AS POSTMASTER GENERAL, THE forty-seven-year-old Montgomery Blair, was to prove himself a splendid administrator of the Post Office Department during the difficult days of the long war. He was even able to improve postal service to a remarkable degree, despite some understandable initial confusion caused by the demonetization of the stamps of 1851–57 and the disruption of the postal routes.

Born in Kentucky, Montgomery Blair was a graduate of West Point and had served as a lieutenant in the Seminole War. He resigned his commission to study law, and settled in 1837 in St. Louis, where he served as mayor and later as judge of the Court of Common Pleas. He left the bench to resume the practice of law, moving to Washington in 1853 to practice before the Supreme Court. President Pierce appointed him the first solicitor for the Court of Claims in 1855, but Buchanan later fired him because of Blair's pronounced antislavery views. Blair's prestige among abolitionists was greatly increased when he became counsel for Dred Scott, the Missouri slave who was suing in the Supreme Court for his freedom, and Blair himself became so attracted by the antislavery plank of the Republican party that he became a Democrat-Republican, attending the Republican convention in Chicago in 1860 as a delegate from Maryland. A tall, spare man, who, despite his determined views, spoke quietly and calmly, Blair was to become unwittingly a controversial figure in the cabinet and a political liability for Lincoln near the end of his first term.

Shortly after the war began, Postmaster General Blair started to formulate plans for closing down the postal service the United States was still providing in the "disloyal states." It was important for these services to be suspended for two reasons. First, and most important to the Post Office Department, there were large stocks of the 1857 issue in post offices throughout the South. If these stamps were secretly transported to the North and sold, the post office would be providing services without getting paid, and the rebellion could be financed from the sale of these stamps. Another consideration was that, if the postal services in the South were disrupted, it would be much more difficult for the rebellion to be organized effectively, because of a lack of adequate communications.

In order to confront the first of these concerns, it was decided to produce a new issue of postage stamps for use in the loyal states, and to demonetize the previous issues, making them useless for the purpose of financing the Confederate cause. The matter of closing down postal services in the South was not so simply dealt with. There were still some people, postmasters included, who lived in the southern states but who were loyal to the Union. To deprive these people of any basic means of communication would not be right. To stop postal services before the opposition had gotten itself properly organized would not be gentlemanly. As a part of the fair play diplomacy which existed at the start of the war, it was decided that the U.S. Post Office Department would continue its service in the South until the end of May 1861. Although the postal services did continue, many of the post offices in the South did not turn over to Washington the money they took in. In one report, Blair noted that 8,535 post offices in the "disloyal states" had made no quarterly returns in the third quarter of the fiscal year, a period running from January to March 1861.

On June 1, 1861, the United States government prohibited the ex-

A colorful Union patriotic cover used from Bristol, Rhode Island, to North Englewood, New Jersey, on July 30, 1861. (R. Meyersburg collection)

change of mail between the North and South, and the Post Office Department ordered its postmasters to deliver any letters from the South to the Dead Letter Office. Montgomery Blair then set about the second phase of this policy, issuing a new set of stamps to replace those then in use. Although there were eventually to be eleven stamps in the issue of 1861, time was of the essence and only those stamps which were needed to satisfy the most common rates, such as the one cent, the three cent, and the five cent, were printed and in use by August of that year. At this time the stamps

Although mail between North and South was officially allowed to follow its normal course until June 1, 1861, some of the border post offices, Washington, D.C., included, stopped southbound letters at least a week earlier. This cover, mailed in New York on May 22, should have arrived at the Washington, D.C., post office on May 23 or 24. Sent to the Dead Letter Office on July 1, 1861, the cover was opened to ascertain the address of the mailer, and was returned to him in New York. The one-cent and three-cent stamps of the 1857 issue paid for carrier service to the mails in New York and postage from New York to the intended Virginia destination. Return postage from the Dead Letter Office was to be collected from the sender, as indicated by the "DUE 3 cts" handstamp. (National Philatelic Collection)

from the issues of 1851 and 1857 were demonetized and were replaced by the new ones. But this replacement was carried out in stages as the new stamps became available, and different schedules of demonetization were established for different parts of the country because of the time required to produce and transport a sufficient supply of new stamps.

In early August, the Post Office Department sent a letter to all postmasters in the loyal states informing them of the new stamps, which "are of a new style, differing both in design and color from those hitherto used,"

Despite the official break in mail service from South to North, there were still several channels through which the mail moved, one being by way of the Louisville Courier Journal *offices in Louisville, Kentucky. Letters sent under separate cover to the offices of this border state newspaper were, if properly franked with U.S. postage, deposited in the Louisville post office, from which they could continue north. This cover followed such a route, originating at a Virginia plantation and transiting the Louisville post office on July 29, 1861. The cover reached Boston on August 1, and was forwarded to Newport, Rhode Island, on the same day. The original three-cent 1857 stamp was accepted for postage, but the forwarding to Newport required an additional three cents, indicated by the "Due 3 cents" handstamp, which was applied at Boston. (National Philatelic Collection)*

and instructing them to place ads in their local newspapers informing people that they should exchange their old stamps for the new ones. This was just a few weeks after the Battle of Bull Run (First Manassas) in Virginia, where the South had won the first major battle of the war, shocking people in the North who had expected a quick and easy victory, and who were now being forced to gird themselves for what promised to be a long and difficult struggle. The postmasters were also instructed to allow a six-day period for the exchange of stamps after the notice appeared in the newspaper; when that

The Adams Express Company provided another means of sending mail from the South to North after the official break in mail services. This cover was mailed at Richmond on August 17, 1861, with ten cents in postage paid, indicating a double-rate letter. Because it was addressed to a northern city, the Confederate post office sent the letter to the offices of the Adams Express Company at Louisville, Kentucky, from which point the letter could be introduced into the northern mails. The Adams Express Company did not perform this service out of the goodness of its heart, and the notation of the fifteen-cent fee charged for this letter is visible through the U.S. postage stamp placed at the upper right corner of the cover. After passing through the Adams office on August 21, the cover was mailed from the Louisville post office on the 22d and reached Boston on August 26, 1861. At Boston, the cover was marked "Due 3 cents." because the Adams office had only put the single-letter-rate postage on this double-weight cover. When it was found that the cover needed to be forwarded to Caldwell, New York, a manuscript "Forwarded 3" was added, and the total postage due of six cents was noted below that. By the end of August 1861, the transfer of the southern mails through Louisville had come to a halt and severe

period expired they were to return all of the old issues of 1851 and 1857 to the Post Office Department. The old stamps were then invalid for use at that office, and postmasters were told to inspect the mail personally to make sure that none of those old stamps were "used through the mail or otherwise."

A schedule was established for this demonetization because it was "impossible to supply all offices with new stamps at once." People residing in Kentucky, Missouri, Illinois, Ohio, Indiana, Maryland, and Pennsylvania *penalties were levied on anyone found to be promoting correspondence with the South without official authorization. (National Philatelic Collection)*

were allowed to use the old stamps until November 1, and postmasters were instructed to deliver any letters sent from those states prior to that date and bearing the earlier issues. December 1 was the date established for demonetization in the "other loyal states east of the Rocky Mountains." And January 1, 1862, was the date for California, Oregon, and the territories of New Mexico, Utah, and Washington.

Although this demonetization of the old stamps was popularly acclaimed in the Union as an aggressive and necessary measure, Montgomery Blair has been criticized because he did it on his own initiative and without an act of Congress. Quite obviously, he discussed it with Lincoln, but the actual demonetization was based solely on directives from Blair. However, it seems that this action was within the province of the postmaster general at that time because the acts of Congress under which he was operating did not restrict him to any particular designs of the stamps he issued, nor did they require him to keep any particular issue in print indefinitely. At any rate, Blair did demonetize the old stamps and he forbade any sale of the new ones to the South, effectively cutting the South out of the U.S. postal system and leaving it with batches of now worthless stamps from the 1851 and 1857 issues.

The demonetization in the North, with its complex schedule of effective dates, caused some confusion during the first months. Sometimes letters bearing the old stamps were marked unpaid by postmasters who received them, even though they were mailed before a particular state's expiration date, apparently because the postmaster did not understand the schedule. At other times the old issues were honored, even though the effective date for the new stamps had passed. As a matter of fact, we find some use of the old stamps after all of the demonetization dates had passed, just as had happened in 1851 when the issue of 1847 was demonetized.

Nevertheless, Montgomery Blair in his report of December 2, 1862, was able to note that by November 9 some 77,117,520 of the new stamps had been issued, as well as 8,939,650 stamped envelopes. He also stated that all Union post offices had by that time been supplied with the new stamps, with the exception of some post offices in Kentucky and Missouri. Blair noted that the old stamps "have been to a great extent counted and destroyed."

A new generation of stamps had been born.

When Montgomery Blair was planning the new issue of stamps in the spring of 1861 he discovered that, fortuitously, the government's printing contract with Toppan, Carpenter for the production of stamps was due to expire that June. This meant that he could put the issue out for bids among a number of contractors. It appears that the bidding for the 1861 issue was much more spirited than when Toppan, Carpenter had submitted its first bid for the contract some ten years earlier. At that time, when stamps were still not compulsory, only about a million and a half stamps were being issued a year, but that number had escalated astronomically to more than 200 million stamps a year by the time the Civil War broke out. The postage stamp contract was now a business deal of major proportions, worthy of careful bidding by large contractors.

This fine patriotic cover, mailed from Philadelphia on September 20, 1861, shows the use of the one-cent and three-cent values of the new 1861 issue used to pay the fee for carrier service to the mails—one cent, in addition to the regular three-cent postage. (R. Meyersburg collection)

Blair had two objectives in the actual manufacture of the new stamps. First, he wanted them produced as quickly as possible, and indeed few issues were ever produced as quickly as the issue of 1861. Second, he wanted the stamps to be clearly recognized as a new issue, not to be confused with the older issues, and to that end, he stated in the bid specifications that the new designs should not have the basic denominations expressed in letters, such as "FIVE CENTS," "TEN CENTS," as was done in the issue of 1857, but they

This splendid college cover from Gettysburg, Pennsylvania, bears a single one-cent stamp, paying the rate for printed circulars. (R. Meyersburg collection)

should now be printed in numerals. Thus a postmaster would be able to tell by one quick glance whether any single stamp was from the old issue or the new issue.

Amazingly, for a contract of such great size, Toppan, Carpenter and Co. was rather listless in its bidding, perhaps figuring that, since it had held the contract for the last ten years without serious complaint, it would receive the next one, too. What the firm submitted in the way of the samples required in the bid specification were merely lay-down proofs of the 1857 issue, with the one change of the new numbers, as required by the specifications. On the other hand, the National Bank Note Company of New York made a handsome presentation, submitting entirely new designs and engravings of nine stamps ranging from one cent to ninety cents. These designs were apparently submitted in the form of complete sheets, gummed and perforated, to resemble the finished product they sought to deliver.

Blair had said in his bid specifications that all the designs would "be submitted to a board of disinterested experts or artists for examination," and his advisers liked the National Bank Note designs, although Blair and his associates indicated a number of minor design changes they wanted in the final version. A number of these changes, accordingly, were made between the stamps submitted for the bid proposal and the stamps which were actually issued in August. What Blair liked even more than the new designs was the fact that the National Bank Note's bid was about 30 percent less than the department had paid for stamps in previous years, and in his annual report of December 1861, he was able to justify the expense of demonetizing one issue of stamps and issuing another by the fact that the cost had been absorbed by the lower price of the new contract. The National Bank Note Company was awarded a six-year contract to produce the new stamps.

The sheets of proposed designs the National Bank Note Company submitted with its contract bid in 1861 have caused a great deal of confusion in philatelic circles because the designs and colors of the proposal sheets are slightly different from the stamps as issued. The first design types, which

The two-cent "Black Jack" was issued in 1863 to cover an increase in the rate for circulars, and to meet the new local postage rate which now replaced the former drop-letter and carrier services. This attractive cover, with its elaborate advertisement for the American Life Insurance Company, shows the use of this popular stamp to pay the new local postage rate. The handstamped "CARRIER" mark in this case merely shows that the cover was handled by a carrier. (R. Meyersburg collection)

came to be known as *"Premières Gravures,"* are, in fact, not real stamps but essays, unaccepted designs for stamps. The ten-cent first design may have found its way into use, because the differences between the proposed design and the final accepted design were so small that, in the interest of producing as many stamps as possible in a short time, the plate prepared for the contract proposal was placed in use until a plate with the slight changes in the design could be produced. The copies of the unaccepted designs, not being actual stamps, were used by National Bank Note as samples of its work, particularly in Europe, where most of the copies we know today were found.

The first of the 1861 stamps began to arrive at post offices around the middle of August 1861, and other stamps of the issue were delivered over subsequent years. As in previous issues, all of these stamps are considered part of the issue of 1861, even though two of them were not issued in that calendar year.

One interesting thing about the issue is that, despite the war, and despite the fact that the almost 9,000 post offices in the Confederacy would not, of course, be selling them, the stamps continued to sell in greater quantities as the war progressed.

As the table on page 169 demonstrates, the sale of stamps dipped slightly in the first year of the war, reflecting the immediate loss of outlets in those almost 9,000 post offices in the Confederacy, but then it began to climb steadily until by the end of the war almost twice as many U.S. stamps were being issued as in the early days of the war.

The stamps of the issue of 1861 were:

One cent. Issued in the middle of August 1861, featuring a profile of Benjamin Franklin after a bust by Houdon, framed by an elliptical design composed of lathework. Issued in a number of shades, notably blue, bright blue, indigo, and ultramarine. The lettering "one cent" appears under the

Use of the "Black Jack" to pay the circular rate is exemplified by this cover with its over-all advertising design for a manufacturer of hay and manure forks. (R. Meyersburg collection)

portrait, but there is a large arabic numeral "1" in each upper corner, according to Blair's specifications, in order to distinguish these stamps from the 1857 issue. This same design was followed in all of the stamps of the issue listed below.

Two cents. Not put into use until July 1863, because the act of 1863 had established a fee of two cents for circulars and drop letters. This stamp—known as the "Black Jack"—features a full-face portrait of Andrew Jack-

Wartime Sales of U.S. Stamps

Year Ending June 30	Postage Stamps Sold	Stamped Envelopes & Wrappers Sold
1860	216,370,660	29,280,025
1861	211,788,518	26,027,300
1862	251,307,105	27,234,159
1863	338,340,385	25,548,750
1864	334,054,610	28,218,800
1865	387,419,455	26,206,175

son, after a portrait by Dodge, which takes up all but a small portion of the stamp.

Three cents. The most popularly used one in the issue because it was the basic stamp for the one-half ounce rate, it was also ready and delivered by the middle of August 1861. A profile portrait of George Washington faces to the left and rests on an oblong tablet of lathework. Colors, pink, rose pink, rose, and rose brown. Nearly one and three-quarter billion of these three-cent stamps were printed.

Five cents. Also issued in August 1861, it features a portrait of Thomas Jefferson resting on a crosshatched elliptical tablet surrounded by a border of lathework. Colors, buff, brown yellow, olive yellow, red brown, and brown.

Ten cents. Available in August 1861, it features the head of George Washington on a hatched ground enclosed by three sets of four stars. Colors, dark green, dark yellow green, deep yellow green, and blue green. (This is the only stamp of the 1861 issue found in more than one type; both the *Premières Gravures* and the altered design were available in post offices.)

Twelve cents. Another August 1861 stamp featuring a portrait of George Washington, on a crosshatched elliptical ground, surrounded to the edge of the stamp by a very fine geometrical design. Colors, black, gray black, and intense black.

Fifteen cents. This stamp, issued in April 1866, is the first to feature Abraham Lincoln. The denomination was to cover registry rates, and the basic rate to France and some other countries. The portrait of Lincoln appears on a cross-hatched elliptical ground; on each side are *faces*, bundles of rods bound together, the symbol of authority in ancient Rome. Issued in black, it has been considered a mourning or memorial stamp for the murdered president. The earliest recorded cover is postmarked April 14, 1866, one year after Lincoln was shot at Ford's Theater.

Twenty-four cents. Available in August 1861, featuring a portrait of George Washington, this is the smallest in the series, enclosed by very fine lathework enclosed by five-pointed stars. Colors, violet, gray lilac, red lilac, brown lilac, blackish violet, and steel blue.

Thirty cents. Again, available in August 1861, featuring a profile of Benjamin Franklin facing to the right and enclosed in a circle surrounded by scrollwork. Colors, orange, deep orange.

Ninety cents. Issued in August 1861, featuring a portrait of George

This advertising cover for Dr. Hawks's Universal Stimulant carried a letter from the proprietor, J.M. Hawks, M.D., to his wife, Esther. Hawks was serving as a surgeon with the Freedman's Relief Commission in Union-occupied Port Royal, South Carolina. (National Philatelic Collection)

Washington on a crosshatched elliptical ground. Colors, blue, pale blue, dark blue, and full blue.

Congress in the summer of 1861 passed acts by which soldiers, sailors, and marines in the service of the United States were allowed to send mail without prepayment, postage being collected from the recipient. Congress also mandated that letters duly posted to military personnel at the place of their last assignment should be forwarded to wherever they were presently stationed with no further charge.

Another special exemption of the war years was the mutual agreement between the Confederacy and the Union which allowed captured military personnel on each side to send "prisoner-of-war letters," which were exchanged at designated points and then delivered by the respective postal service in either the Confederacy or the Union to the addressee. These letters were subject to censorship before being passed on to the opposing side. The captured soldier wrote the words "prisoner of war," or something similar, on the envelope to indicate this special category of letter. In addition, there were also "flag-of-truce" letters for civilians sent under the same conditions and with the same censorship, but this practice was not greatly encouraged.

One of the most interesting postally related developments of the Civil War era was the production and use of patriotic envelopes in both the North and South. These privately produced items displayed a wide variety of patriotic symbols on the envelope, which a correspondent could use to "show the colors" while sending messages through the mail. Portraits of Lincoln, Jefferson Davis, and war heroes of both sides, as well as flags and scenes of battles won or lost, were popular subjects for the patriotic artists who produced these items. The examples of "patriotic covers" which have survived remain as eloquent testimony to the deeply felt patriotic sentiments on both sides during that "war of brothers."

Although France was one of the more common foreign destinations for U.S. mails, the 1861 issue at first did not include a stamp which, alone, could pay the fifteen-cent rate then in force. On this cover a five-cent and a ten-cent stamp are used to make up the rate to France. Mailed in July 1862, the cover was routed via the Cunard Line ship Scotia, *resulting in a twelve-cent credit to France in accordance with the postal treaty of 1857. (R. Meyersburg collection)*

Montgomery Blair did a truly remarkable job as postmaster general during those war years—improving service, making innovations, and reducing the postal deficit. This was not the case in the South, as we shall see, but of course a major part of Blair's success was based on the fact that the actual fighting during the war was done largely in the Confederacy itself. Exceptions were those occasional forays by Confederate armies to attack northern cities at the more southerly points of the Union, always eventually repulsed—such as General Lee's abortive march north in 1863 when his Army of Northern Virginia encountered General Mead's Army of the Potomac at Gettysburg. Blair, therefore, was not operating a mail system in a war-ravaged territory overrun with battling armies, but rather he was centered in a relatively stable and prosperous area. There were, of course, occasional guerrilla raids by the Confederates on Union postal routes—such as the raids on the Hannibal-St. Joseph route—but these never seriously or permanently damaged the routes.

Furthermore, Blair began his tenure with an established and functioning postal system, which he then developed and improved, whereas the South, after it was cut off by the Union, had to organize its own postal system, establish rates, and issue stamps for the first time. For Blair, the Confederacy represented a loss of only eleven states with a population of nine million people, more than one third of whom were slaves and mostly illiterate, while his postal system served the twenty-three states of the Union, which had a population of nearly twenty-two million people, most of them free.

Blair had become an astute student of the British postal system, and in his report for the fiscal year of 1862 he compared the two systems, noting

The combination of a three-cent and a twelve-cent stamp was also used to make up the rate for mail to France, as seen on this July 11, 1866, cover from New York to Paris. As with the previously illustrated cover, this one was carried by a British ship, the Java, and the credit of twelve cents was made in France in accordance with the treaty of 1857. The inscription at the top of the cover indicates that the mailbags destined for France remained sealed during their transit of Britain and incurred no British postal fees, thus "French closed mail." (R. Meyersburg collection)

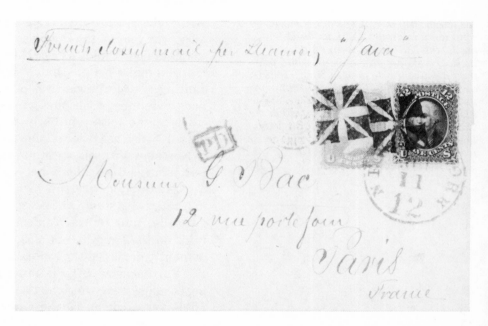

one element of the British system lacking in his and which he wanted to institute: the career service of experienced people in the postal system. He observed that postal employees in Britain were carefully recruited and evaluated before hiring, and that they then tended to make a life-long career out of the service. On the other hand, in America, he noted that in the fiscal year ending June 30, 1862, more than 5,000 of his 19,973 postal employees

The fifteen-cent Lincoln stamp was added to the series of 1861 in the spring of 1866. This denomination allowed payment of the rate to France (fifteen cents per ¼ oz. via French mail) with a single stamp. This cover to France was mailed from the Smithsonian Institution in Washington, D.C., on July 29, 1868. (National Philatelic Collection)

had left the postal service—2,902 by resignation and another 2,786 by firing. This was 28 percent of his whole force, and it was disruptive to the efficient delivery of the mail. Blair's goal was "the retention of good officers," and the "discharge of incompetent incumbents."

As the mail increased during the war, Blair also sought to establish new internal procedures for moving it quickly and efficiently. He appointed special agents to speed the distribution of mail at critical points, such as New York, Cleveland, and Cairo, Illinois, and by the end of his term he had

An interesting feature of the United States transatlantic rates of this period is that a letter mailed to England via British mail packet required nine cents more in postage than a letter to France via British packet that transited England on the way to its destination. All the same, there was no choice. If one needed to send a letter to England, the rate was twenty-four cents— and many people did need to send letters to England. This cover (front and reverse) is unusual in that it shows transatlantic use of a patriotic cover. A British packet carried the cover from Boston, resulting in a credit of nineteen cents to Britain on this 1861 cover. (R. Meyersburg collection)

developed a new system of nationwide distribution which had streamlined the postal delivery system.

Blair lobbied Congress for the new rates included in the act of March 3, 1863, which repealed the ten-cent over-the-Rockies charge, which had been put into effect just a few weeks before the war, and which for the first time

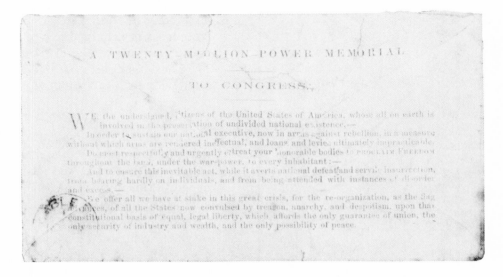

A TWENTY MILLION POWER MEMORIAL

TO CONGRESS.

WE, the undersigned, citizens of the United States of America, whose all on earth is involved in the preservation of undivided national existence,—

In order to sustain our national executive, now in arms against rebellion, in a measure without which arms are rendered ineffectual, and loans and levies ultimately impracticable,

Do most respectfully and urgently entreat your honorable bodies to PROCLAIM FREEDOM throughout the land, under the war-power, to every inhabitant:—

And to ensure this inevitable act, while it averts national defeat and servile insurrection, from bearing hardly on individuals, and from being attended with instances of disorder and excess,—

We offer all we have at stake in this great crisis, for the re-organization, as the flag implies, of all the States now convulsed by treason, anarchy, and despotism, upon that constitutional basis of equal, legal liberty, which affords the only guarantee of union, the only security of industry and wealth, and the only possibility of peace.

established an actual uniform rate for the whole country. Henceforth, all letters up to one-half ounce would be carried for three cents, regardless of distance. Blair called it "the lowest postage hitherto adopted by any government." The act also established a rate of two cents per half ounce for drop letters, requiring the issuance of the two-cent stamp mentioned earlier.

In addition, the act of 1863 divided mail into three classes, and established rate scales for them. First class was letter mail; second class was regularly issued publications; and third class was all other mail. The rates for printed matter were simplified and reduced—weekly newspapers, for instance, were charged five cents per four ounces. A general weight limit of four pounds per mailable article was also established.

These new rates became effective everywhere in the Union and in the territories on July 1, 1863.

The act of 1863 also empowered Blair to establish another major improvement in the postal delivery system, a free letter carrier service "for the delivery of letters in the places respectively where post-offices are established." Prior to this time, most of the mail was presented at the post office and picked up there, but Blair was now authorized to hire mail carriers at a salary "not exceeding $800 per annum" as a part of the regular postal service. From this point onward, the separate carrier and postal systems discussed earlier became one.

Most of the carrier offices were initially located in the northeastern quarter of the country, although Louisville, Kentucky, was also included in the system. By September 1863, Blair was able to report that "in the City of New York there are now, daily, five depositories [letter boxes] in the various parts of the city." New York City employed 137 carriers, and Philadelphia 119, but Chicago did not see its first carriers until the following year. By 1864, delivery service had been established in sixty-six cities, and some 685 letter carriers were employed by the post office.

Yet another improvement in the Union mail system was the domestic money order, which was authorized by the act of May 17, 1864. As mentioned earlier, internal theft was a problem which had plagued the department for some time, and although the registry system introduced in 1855 did offer some control, it did not address the fundamental matter of the actual cash that was carried in those envelopes.

That question became even more critical during the war when families were sending monies to the Union soldiers on the battlefronts, and the system devised in 1864 was basically designed to safeguard transmissions of small amounts of money by issuing vouchers redeemable by the recipient. A survey at the Dead Letter Office in Washington had revealed that the average amount of money enclosed in a letter in 1864 was $5.18; accordingly, the act provided money orders from one dollar to thirty dollars. The fees for this service were modest: ten cents for amounts up to ten dollars, fifteen cents for up to twenty dollars, and twenty cents for up to thirty dollars.

This service was initially introduced at some 141 larger post offices, but it was eventually extended to virtually all offices, branches, and stations in the Union. By 1865, at the end of the war, the domestic money orders issued annually amounted to $1,360,122—and thus a large amount of "money mail" had been removed from the system.

What was even more remarkable about the large improvements Montgomery Blair had instituted in the postal system during the war was the fact

The ninety-cent denomination of the 1861 issue is quite scarce on covers, only about fifty examples being known. This cover to France is franked with a single ninety-cent stamp intended as a six-times-rate payment. Sent from New Orleans on December 22, 1866, the cover was carried to New York for placement on a transatlantic steamer. The foreign division clerk who handled the cover in New York rated it as being a five-times-rate cover and marked the face with a sixty-cent credit to France. The ninety-cent prepayment was thus a fifteen-cent overpayment of the proper seventy-five-cent rate. The cover was put on the French packet St. Laurent, *leaving New York on December 29, and arriving at Le Havre, France, on January 9, 1867. (Photo from the files of R. Meyersburg)*

that he was able to offer these extra services while at the same time reducing the deficit. In the year before Blair became postmaster general, the department had sustained losses of more than six million dollars, but at the end of his first full year in office that deficit had been reduced by more than half to less than three million dollars. In 1863 the deficit was further reduced to about 150,000 and in 1864 it was 202,000. Finally, in 1865, as we have noted, there was the single year of a post office profit of almost one million dollars. Improved and less expensive service, therefore, was not producing staggering deficits, and Montgomery Blair was demonstrating the validity of the postal predictions Rowland Hill had made over a quarter of a century earlier.

In addition to his extremely successful management of the Post Office Department, Montgomery Blair was an active and vocal member of Lincoln's cabinet, advising him on such matters as the timing of the Emancipation Proclamation in 1862. He was very much involved in the Trent affair when two Confederate diplomats headed for Europe were taken off the British mail packet *Trent* (which had been stopped by a Union war vessel) and were placed in a prison in Boston. The British protested strongly, and there was even talk of war, but Blair, the lawyer and former jurist, advised Lincoln that the capture of the two Confederate diplomats off a British ship on the high seas was clearly illegal. Lincoln followed this advice, freeing the two diplomats, who proceeded on to Europe, where they remained for the rest of the war, vainly trying to win military allies for the South. Blair was also touched by the actual violence of the war in July 1864, when Confederate troops led by Jubal Early raided the outskirts of Washington, burning to the ground Blair's house in Maryland. Blair had fled the raid, however, and neither he nor his family was injured.

That same summer of 1864 Blair was embroiled in controversy within his own political party. As the war was drawing to a close and the outcome seemed certain, plans for the Reconstruction period were being discussed in

Washington, and Blair was making pleas for moderation and reconciliation in dealing with the soon-to-be-defeated Confederacy. However, there were strong and loud opposing factions of both the Radical Republicans and Radical Democrats who wanted retribution and indemnification and even prison terms or death for the Confederate leaders. To these radicals, the moderate and articulate Blair in the Lincoln cabinet was a source of intense irritation.

Abraham Lincoln—more sainted in memory than he was at the time—was finding Blair to be a political liability during his campaign for reelection in the fall of 1864. Lincoln, of course, shared Blair's sentiments, as he was to proclaim them in his "malice toward none" statements in his Second Inaugural Address, but he was waging a hard election campaign against Democrat George McClellan and he was under strong pressure from the Radical Republicans to dump Blair from his cabinet and unite the party for the campaign. Remembering that no incumbent president had been reelected since 1832, Lincoln on September 22 called Blair to his office and asked for his resignation. Blair's biographer writes that he resigned "cheerfully," and continued to work loyally for Lincoln after leaving office. Thus, one of the most successful and attractive postmasters general in the department's entire history was let go on grounds of political expediency. In his place, Lincoln appointed William Dennison, a forty-eight-year-old former governor of Ohio and the chairman of the Republican National Convention at Baltimore in June of that year.

Montgomery Blair turned over the Post Office Department to his successor in excellent shape, and when he left office in that fall of 1864 the war

This beautiful Bible verse cover was mailed by a Confederate soldier held prisoner at the Fort Delaware prison camp. Mail departing from the camps was carefully examined for information on military actions as well as suggestions of poor treatment or planned escapes. After examination, the cover was struck with an oval handstamp reading "PRISONER'S LETTER FORT DELAWARE, DEL./EXAMINED" and given to the post office at Delaware City for mailing. This cover was addressed to William C. Rives [Jr.] in Boston (the son of a former United States official turned Confederate statesman of the same name), who had remained in the North during the war. He corresponded frequently with prisoners in Union camps, and on this cover he dockets having replied on October 29, 1864, "$5 & P.O. stamps enclosed." (National Philatelic Collection)

"Thy God shall be my God."
RUTH I. 16.

was entering its final stages. Lincoln was indeed reelected in November, and by that time those heady Confederate victories of the first year of the war had long passed. The horribly bloody battles of Shiloh, Antietam, and Gettysburg had now also become cruel memories in a war which would see some 620,000 soldiers killed. The Confederacy was tottering, as the Union General Ulysses Grant led his Army of the Potomac toward the South for the final and ultimately successful campaign to take Richmond, the capital of the Confederacy. As part of that campaign, Grant had dispatched General

David G. Hunter with his blue-coated soldiers into the Shenandoah Valley "to eat up Virginia clear and clean as far as you can go, so that crows flying over it for the balance of this season will have to carry their provender with them." The Confederate General Beauregard, who had boldly stormed Fort Sumter in 1861, stated sadly in 1864 that "the last hour of the Confederacy has arrived."

XI Stamps of the Confederate States of America, 1861–1865

AS THE SECESSION MOVEMENT GAINED MOMENTUM IN THE WINTER of 1860–61, six states joined South Carolina in its break from the Union, passed acts of secession, and assumed the status of independent states. It was soon clear that an association of these independent states under one government was necessary if the southern states were to be successful in their flight from northern domination. A provisional Congress was convened at Montgomery, Alabama, and a new nation, the Confederate States of America (C.S.A.), was born on February 8, 1861.

Jefferson Davis, the newly elected president of the C.S.A., saw the establishment of an efficient postal service as a vital factor in the development of his country. For the important post of postmaster general, Davis approached John H. Reagan, a Texas lawyer and jurist well known for his administrative abilities. At first, Reagan declined the appointment, but after considerable appeal to his patriotic spirit, he agreed to accept the job. From the time of his appointment in March 1861, until the fall of the Confederacy in the spring of 1865, Reagan was fighting a losing battle to establish and maintain an effective postal service. Unlike Montgomery Blair, his counterpart in the North, Reagan had to run the Confederate postal service through land that was often a battleground and along coasts and rivers that were effectively blockaded. The only period of grace during John Reagan's tenure as the Confederacy's postmaster general was from the time of his appointment until the end of May 1861. During this period, as we have previously mentioned, the U.S. postal system continued to function in the southern states and U.S. postage stamps continued to serve for the payment of postal fees.

The use of U.S. postage stamps in the Confederate States continued until June 1, 1861, and resulted in some ironic consequences, such as this May 15, 1861, cover addressed to the Hon. William C. Rives, Member of Congress, Montgomery, Alabama. The U.S. mails, in this instance, carried a message to the rebel congress, which was then in session. The three-cent stamp of the 1857 issue is canceled with the station handstamp of Cobham on the Virginia Central Railroad. Covers showing railroad cancels on U.S. stamps used in the Confederate States are quite scarce. (National Philatelic Collection)

Starting on June 1, 1861, the C.S.A. postal service was on its own. No postage stamps were available, so postmasters reverted to the early practice of collecting postage in cash and marking the amount paid with either pen or handstamped markings. Some postmasters, no doubt remembering the time before the issue of any stamps in America, prepared their own provisional stamps for local use, much in the manner of the earlier postmasters' provisional issues discussed in chapter 4.

The Confederate postal service had to be built almost from the ground up, with routes and rates being established, transportation being contracted for, and stamps being produced for the first time. Knowing that his early expenses would be high, and mindful of the insistence of the C.S.A. Congress that the mail service must be self-supporting, Reagan set the postage rates at five cents per half ounce for letters going less than 500 miles, ten cents for greater distances, and two cents for drop letters. Even though these rates were a considerable increase over those being charged in the North at the same time, the runaway inflation which accompanied the deterioration of the Confederate economy led to a doubling of the basic letter rate to ten cents within one year.

Because the largest part of the American printing industry was located in the North, and thus could not be called upon to print the postal issues of the newly formed Confederate States, the initial contract for stamps was made with Thomas De La Rue & Company, a firm with offices in London. Ironically, the great delays in the production and the transatlantic shipment of this issue (including the capture of the first shipment by the Union blockade) led to the introduction of domestically printed stamps as the first C.S.A. issue. The Richmond firm of Hoyer and Ludwig was chosen to provide postage stamps while the De La Rue issue was being prepared in England. The first issue of the C.S.A. was composed of three stamps which appeared starting in October 1861. This issue was rather poorly lithographed in the following designs:

This seven-star-flag Confederate patriotic cover was produced between early March and May of 1861, when Virginia was admitted as the eighth state of the Confederacy. The five-cent postage was paid with a Memphis, Tennessee, postmaster's provisional stamp. The rate indicates that the cover was mailed sometime after the beginning of June 1861 when the new Confederate rates went into effect. After reaching New Orleans, the cover was advertised in the paper as being at the post office. This advertising service is indicated by the boxed "ADV." handstamp at top center. (National Philatelic Collection)

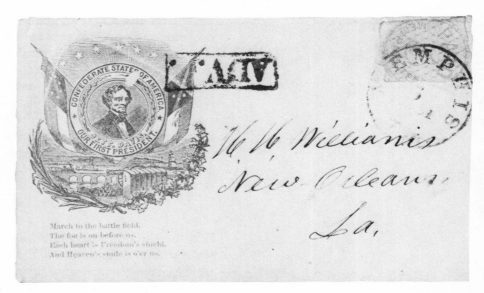

Two cents. Issued early in 1862, featuring a portrait of Andrew Jackson in an oval frame with scrollwork around the frame. The words "CONFEDERATE STATES" are printed in a circular fashion around the top of the frame. Color, green.

Five cents. A portrait of Jefferson Davis in an oval frame with scrollwork outside it. The words "CONFEDERATE STATES OF AMERICA" are inside the frame over Davis's head; at the top is "POSTAGE"; at the bottom, "FIVE CENTS."

Color, green.

Ten cents. Another of the 1861 lithographs, this one features a portrait of Thomas Jefferson in a bordered oval frame with a considerable amount of writing on it: "CONFEDERATE STATES OF AMERICA" in the frame's border, "POSTAGE" on top, "TEN CENTS" at the bottom, and the arabic numeral "10" in each of the four corners. Color, blue.

The five- and ten-cent designs were later produced in different colors (five-cent in blue, ten-cent in rose). At one point, the stamps were printed by the T.C. Paterson Company, and these were issued in mid-1862.

～～～

The first of the stamps from De La Rue arrived safely from London in April 1862. They were placed on sale and the plate, which had also been shipped from England, was given to the Richmond firm of Archer and Daly for further printings. Only the five-cent De La Rue stamps had arrived in the C.S.A. They, and the locally produced stamps made from the same plate, feature a portrait of Jefferson Davis set in a circular frame within a square ornamented with a star in each corner. The words "CONFEDERATE STATES" appear at the top; "FIVE CENTS" is at the bottom within solid labels. Color, blue.

Only two months after the stamps from De La Rue were put into service, the basic letter rate was changed from five to ten cents. A new issue of engraved postage stamps was planned, and since the ten-cent value of the lithographed issue was in short supply, most people used two copies of the five-cent typographed stamps to make up the ten-cent rate.

The two five-cent stamps used to make up the ten-cent letter rate on this July 15, 1862, cover are in distinctly different shades of green. The cover was mailed at Charlottesville, Virginia, and traveled only to nearby Cobham Depot, a short distance for the new ten-cent rate of postage. (National Philatelic Collection)

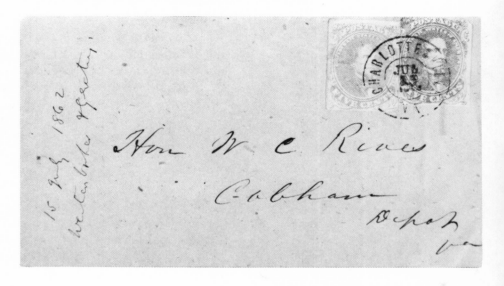

The Archer and Daly firm was chosen to produce the new engraved postage stamp issue. Plans called for three stamps: a new two-cent value for drop letters and circulars, a ten-cent value for the standard letter rate, and a twenty-cent stamp to cover heavy letters and the trans-Mississippi rate of forty cents which, of course, required two stamps. The designs of these new adhesives were:

Two cents. Andrew Jackson in an oval frame surrounded with scroll-work. The word "POSTAGE" appears in a solid label at the top, with "TWO

CENTS" at the bottom. This is the only Confederate postage stamp which does not have the words "CONFEDERATE STATES" or "C.S.A." included somewhere in the design, although the initials "C" and "S" do appear in small shields in the lower corners. Color, reddish brown.

Ten cents. Four distinct types of the ten-cent stamps were printed by Archer and Daly. The main design—a portrait of Jefferson Davis in an oval frame surrounded with scrollwork—was common to each, as was the lettering "POSTAGE" in a solid label at the top, and "THE CONFEDERATE STATES OF AMERICA" split into two labels to the right and left of the central portrait. At first the stamps were printed with the words "TEN CENTS" in a label at the bottom. This inscription was later changed to "10 CENTS," and the second design was produced in three varieties: first, with a rectangular frame outside each of the stamp designs, second, with no frame lines, and third with slightly modified scrollwork and a wavy frame line close to the design. The color for all four types was blue, a wide variety of shades being found.

Twenty cents. A portrait of George Washington in an oval frame with a scrollwork arch above and looped ribbons below. The arabic numeral "20" appears at top center, flanked by "THE CONFEDERATE STATES OF AMERICA." The ribbon at the bottom is inscribed "POSTAGE TWENTY CENTS." Color, green.

The ten-cent stamps of the last two types mentioned above were later printed from the same plates by the firm of Keating and Ball in Columbia, South Carolina. This transfer of plates was necessitated by circumstances we shall discuss later. The Keating and Ball stamps are easily recognizable because of their low-quality printing and dark-blue ink.

An additional stamp in the denomination of one cent was printed in

1862, but was never issued because the low rate was never in effect. This typographed stamp features a portrait of John C. Calhoun in a circular frame ornamented in the same manner as the De La Rue issue of 1862, of which this would have become a part. Color, light orange.

In the early days of the war, the southern mails moved with a fair degree of efficiency. The few railroads within the Confederacy were used to best advantage, transporting both troops and mail at an admirable rate. In the spirit of patriotism so common in the early days of the new nation, many of the expenses of running the rail companies were absorbed by the stockholders rather than being billed to the government, even though the loss of equipment was largely due to enemy action against troop trains and military supply transports. John Reagan was also able to take advantage of public generosity, getting many of his postal contracts at reduced rates.

Those were the days of high hopes, when gray-clad Confederate soldiers were charging successfully against Union forces, shouting their famous "rebel yell," a high-pitched wailing scream which a Union soldier described as "nothing like it this side of the infernal region." But then the superior resources and the overwhelming manpower of the North began to take their toll, and the important communications centers of the South started to fall into Union hands—such as New Orleans and Nashville in 1862. The fall of such strategic cities severely disrupted the orderly flow of mail.

The most serious disruption yet occurred in 1863 with the capture of

Two copies of the five-cent stamps printed in Richmond from the De La Rue plates make up the ten-cent rate on this thirteen-star patriotic cover used from Richmond to Summerfield, Alabama. (National Philatelic Collection)

Port Hudson and Vicksburg on the Mississippi, after which Lincoln exulted that "the Father of Waters again goes unvexed to the sea." Union forces had now gained control of the Mississippi and the river had become a Union highway which cut off regular east-west mail service for the Confederacy. To get mail across the Mississippi, Reagan in 1863 resorted to letting out special Confederate government contracts to daring people who would run the Union blockades and dodge troops to cross with the mail. The service was offered twice a week, and the charge was forty cents per half ounce of mail, which was a bargain considering the extreme dangers of the route where the expressmen had to cross enemy lines.

Reagan established alternate Confederate mail terminals at either Meridian or Brandon in Mississippi on one side of the river, and at either Shreveport or Alexandria in Louisiana on the other side, and the expressmen made their pickups and deliveries at those terminals. These fearless mail couriers stayed off the main routes to evade Union troops and they followed bridle paths and cattle tracks, which often led them through swampy wilderness areas until they reached the river's edge. Then they stealthily rowed their skiffs across the river under the cover of darkness, maneuvering them carefully between the patrolling Union gunboats until they reached the other side, where they continued their furtive journey on land again until they arrived at the Confederate terminal and delivered the mail. It was a bold, daring, outrageous express mail service, but it was a far cry from the regular, orderly service Montgomery Blair was offering in the North.

〰️

As the war dragged on, not only were the great southern cities beginning to fall, but incredible destruction was being wreaked on the South, which affected the very materials needed to send the mail. In May 1864 Gen. William Tecumseh Sherman began his brutal march through Georgia. With his 100,000 seasoned veterans he started out for Atlanta opposed only by 53,000 ill-equipped troops of Gen. Joseph Johnston's Army of Tennessee. It took

This cover probably originated in the North and was sent under separate cover to Saunders & Son, a forwarding agency in Nassau, Bahamas. The forwarding agent gave the cover to one of the fast ships we now know as "blockade runners" for transport to the Confederate shore. When the cover arrived at Wilmington, North Carolina, it was rated as a twelve-cent ship letter. Two cents of this amount went to the captain of the ship that brought the letter to port, and the remaining ten cents paid the Confederate postage from Wilmington to Savannah, Georgia. (National Philatelic Collection)

Sherman seventy-four days to travel the one hundred miles to Atlanta and he captured the city on September 2. Leaving Atlanta behind him in flames, he set out again on November 1 on his "march to the sea," cutting a swath of devastation, destruction, and ravage fifty miles wide. On December 22, Sherman reached the sea, and telegraphed Lincoln, "I beg to present you, as a Christmas gift, the city of Savannah." What Sherman had done was to bisect the Deep South.

The South—now bisected and dissected within, and severely blockaded

This homemade envelope was constructed from wallpaper, clearly indicating the basic shortages which crippled the Confederacy during the final years of the war. The cover was mailed from Georgetown to Columbia, South Carolina. (National Philatelic Collection)

without—began to experience dire shortages of basic commodities in 1864 and 1865, including, of course, postal materials. Stamps were in short supply, and some postmasters were either handstamping the letters or offering some kind of provisionals. Patriotic covers had almost disappeared, because envelopes themselves had become so scarce. Envelopes were used twice, and an imaginative variety of homemade envelopes began to appear, constructed from such materials as ledger paper and even wallpaper. The Confederate postal system was on the verge of collapse. As fears grew that the northern armies would soon capture, or completely isolate, the capital city of Richmond, the stamp production process was transferred from Richmond to Columbia, South Carolina, in 1864.

ᔜᔜ

Mercifully, the war was all over in early 1865. Sherman, after resting for a month, proceeded north to join forces with Grant, who was still unable to dislodge the tenacious Lee from Richmond. Now realizing that Richmond was no longer defensible, Lee so informed Jefferson Davis, who then moved the Confederate capital to Danville, Virginia, near the North Carolina border. But Robert E. Lee, that bravest and wisest of generals, who had both pilloried and eluded Union forces for almost four years, was not through yet: he planned to march out of Richmond and regroup at Danville. His once proud Army of Northern Virginia, which had numbered 76,000 men in its glory days, was in 1865 reduced to 35,000 ragged and poorly equipped soldiers, now hotly pursued by 80,000 Union troops with full materiel. Lee's forces were entrapped and encircled near the village of Appomattox Courthouse in central Virginia, and he was forced to surrender to General Grant. Appomattox was the effective end of the war. Even though skirmishes continued for some time and Jefferson Davis himself was not captured until May 10, Lee's surrender marked the true end of the four-year conflict.

On April 9, 1865, the gray-clad Confederate soldiers at Appomattox began stacking their arms in front of the Union ranks, and a Union officer from Maine wrote of the scene in a poignant and frequently-quoted narrative. He said there was absolute silence, and no cheering or sounds of trumpets or rolls of drums, only "an awed stillness rather, and breath-holding, as if it were the passing of the dead."

XII Issues of the Reconstruction: the First Federal Pictorials

LESS THAN TWO WEEKS LATER LINCOLN WAS DEAD, FELLED BY ASSAS-sin John Wilkes Booth, and he was succeeded by his vice-president, Andrew Johnson of Tennessee. Unlike his predecessors, Johnson did not change his cabinet, although Montgomery Blair advised him to do so, and thus William Dennison continued as postmaster general during those crucial days of postal reconstruction which followed the war.

Despite the politically tainted nature of the circumstances surrounding his appointment, Dennison had one important qualification that would help him during that time of reorganization: he had been a successful business-man in Ohio before entering politics, particularly in transportation and banking. With such a background, he developed into an extremely effective postmaster general.

His first successes were in the North, where he cleared out the huge blacklog of mail which had built up during the war. Despite Blair's an-nounced intention of breaking off postal relations with the South, people still astonishingly continued to address letters to southern post offices throughout the war, and these letters were now piled up in the Dead Letter Office. Turning to the South, Dennison had to refurbish the deteriorated mail service there and reintegrate it into the United States postal system. By November 15, 1865, just a few months after the war's end, Dennison had 241 mail routes operating along 18,640 miles in areas which had formerly been part of the Confederate States of America.

There had been 8,902 post offices in the South prior to the war, but by November 1865 only 3,234 of them had been restored to the federal system and were listed in the U.S. Auditor's report as "reestablished." In fact, many

The great backlog of mail which had accumulated by the end of the war was largely caused by the rapidly changing addresses of people who lived in the war-torn areas of the South. This cover was mailed in June 1863 to Ezra Bartlett, M.D., in Union-occupied Memphis, Tennessee. Dr. Bartlett was not to be found, and when he failed to answer two advertisements for the letter, it was marked "Not Found" and sent to the Dead Letter Office, where it was received on October 14, 1863. At the Dead Letter Office, the cover was slit open and the name of the sender was noted on the end on the envelope. The cover was returned to the sender marked "DUE 6" to cover postage from Memphis to the Dead Letter Office and then back to Haverhill, New Hampshire. As the war neared its end, the facilities of the Dead Letter Office were strained beyond its capacity to perform, and the mail backed up in huge piles. (National Philatelic Collection)

of the prewar post offices in the South would never be restored, mainly because they were no longer needed in the improved postal system Blair had developed or because they were single-person operations and the local postmaster had died and no one else was interested or willing to take his place. By 1867 all post offices started in the South were no longer listed as "reestablished," but simply as "new." By that year, there were 25,163 U.S. post offices, including both those in the North and the South. This was about 3,000 fewer than the total number of post offices in the whole nation before the war.

Financially, Dennison's Post Office Department showed a deficit of a little over one million dollars in 1867, the first full fiscal year after the war. By the following year, when there was a new postmaster general, the deficit had risen to about four million dollars, although the revenues were at an all-time high of more than fifteen million dollars. The issuance of stamps was at an all-time high too—in 1867 there had been issued 371,599,605 stamps and 63,086,650 stamped envelopes, all of that same issue of 1861.

∿∿∿

One of the methods William Dennison developed in 1865 to move the huge backup of mail was the Railway Mail Service, a concept which had been discussed and even tested for some time. The railroad itself was entering into a new era in which it would become the main mode of mail transportation, replacing the old stagecoaches and steamboats. As an indication of this shift, Montgomery Blair in 1863 began to delete from his annual report the notation of how many route miles of mail were carried by stagecoach each year, lumping those miles instead in a catch-all category of mails carried with "Certainty, celerity, and security," a secondary category to the growing number of route miles for railroads.

As far back as 1837, the Post Office Department had employed route agents on some railroads who rode the trains, accepting mail en route and doing basic sorting of it. However, this mail sorting en route was minimal, and what the route agent usually did for all mail beyond the end of his line

George B. Armstrong, first superintendent of the Railway Mail Service.

was to pouch it together for delivery to what were called Distributing Post Offices (D.P.O.'s). The D.P.O. system had been established back in 1810, and by the beginning of the Civil War there were some fifty of them across the nation serving as major redistribution centers where the mail was sorted again and then forwarded to post offices in the D.P.O.'s area.

Understandably a large amount of mail arriving at each D.P.O. was held up until it could be sorted, and during the Civil War some imaginative local postmasters had experimented to see if the mails could be expedited if sorting was done in transit aboard trains, thus allowing for immediate distribution as soon as the mail arrived at the D.P.O. With Montgomery Blair's full authorization, an experiment was conducted in 1862 by William Douglas, an assistant postmaster at St. Joseph, Missouri. He boarded the Hannibal & St. Joseph Railroad in Palmyra, and en route to St. Joseph he opened the pouches and personally sorted the California mail, a task that ordinarily would have been done at the St. Joseph D.P.O. Thus, when the mail arrived, it was immediately forwarded without being delayed at the D.P.O.

The concept was further articulated by George B. Armstrong, who was in charge of the Chicago post office and who thought that the some 370 route agents could be put to work on the trains to make them "traveling post offices." Armstrong submitted his plan in writing to the Post Office Department in Washington, and he was allowed to implement it on August 28, 1864, when he placed the first "Railway Post Office" (R.P.O.) car in operation between Chicago and Clinton, Iowa, on the Chicago & Northwestern Railroad.

Armstrong's plan seemed to work remarkably well, and Dennison put it into full operation as the war was ending. In his report of November 15, 1865, he was able to state that "Railway post offices have been established on several leading railroads." He also said that arrangements were being made for their introduction on other lines, and he predicted that it would accelerate the mail and also reduce the number of D.P.O.'s, since the main job of sorting would now be done en route.

Dennison was correct in his predictions, and other refinements were added to the Railway Mail Service, such as the use of trackside cranes to exchange mail "on the fly" on nonstop runs. Also, some lines used specially constructed forty-foot R.P.O. cars, which were fully equipped to serve as those "traveling post offices." The Railway Mail Service, accelerating the mail considerably and unblocking the distribution centers, was a major breakthrough in the U.S. postal system.

The other postmasters general who had served during the war on opposite sides of the conflict were never to involve themselves in postal matters again after the war. Montgomery Blair returned to his rebuilt Maryland house in what is today Silver Spring, and he practiced law and was a powerful adviser to presidents for the rest of his life.

John Henninger Reagan, the Confederate postmaster general, was, as a Confederate cabinet officer, arrested in 1865 (he had also served in a dual role as secretary of the C.S.A. Treasury during the last few weeks of the war) and he was imprisoned for several months at Fort Warren in Boston Harbor. On May 28, 1865, he wrote a moving letter to President Johnson, urging the wisdom and justice of a lenient attitude toward the people of the South, which seemed to have played a large part in framing Johnson's attitude during that difficult time. Reagan was later to return to Washington as a member of the House of Representatives and a United States Senator from Texas.

More controversial was Joseph Holt, U.S. postmaster general immediately prior to the war, who was to continue in his role of judge-advocate after the war when he was the prosecutor in the Lincoln assassination trial in which Mary Surratt and three other "conspirators" were condemned to death and executed. Holt, who was accused of suppressing evidence, had become the darling of both the vengeful Radical Democrats and the Republicans during and after the war. He remained judge-advocate until 1875, and during his years of retirement spoke and wrote in defense of his activities during the Surratt trial.

William Dennison's successful short career as postmaster general came to an end in 1866 when, expressing dissatisfaction with Andrew Johnson's policies, he resigned and returned to his business interests in Ohio. Johnson appointed in his place Alexander Randall, a forty-three-year-old former governor of Wisconsin. This was to prove to be an excellent appointment, mainly because of Randall's own personal experience in the U.S. postal service. As a young man of twenty-six, he had been the local postmaster in the village of Prairieville, Wisconsin, and after his term as governor, Lincoln

appointed him minister to Rome. Following his tour of duty abroad, Randall returned to Washington, where Lincoln made him first assistant postmaster general in 1863, a position he held at the time of his appointment as postmaster general. The appointment was also personally gratifying to Johnson because Randall was to become one of Johnson's most staunch and ardent supporters during the stormy days of early 1868, when impeachment proceedings were brought against the President.

Randall, the experienced postal official, continued the innovative policies of his predecessors, notably the development of the free carrier service system started by Blair, and in his report of November 1867, he noted that this type of free delivery "continues to grow in public favor." He said that the Post Office Department's experience to date justified the belief that "it will supersede the present system of box delivery, increase correspondence, especially in large cities, and not only pay its expenses, but yield a revenue to the department."

But Randall, with his insider's information, also turned his attention to another matter which had been of concern to postal officials for some time: the problem of "washing" or "cleaning" stamps, by which the cancellation mark could be removed and the stamp used again. It is uncertain just how widespread this practice was at the time, because very few washed stamps have survived, but for many years it was a matter of concern to the post office, and whether the problem was real or merely feared, there were a number of proposed solutions during the war, none of which really seemed satisfactory. During that period, postal workers canceled stamps either in pen and ink or with a handstamp, and some way was being sought to prevent people from removing those markings with an ink eradicator.

In 1867 Alexander Randall thought he had found such a solution, and in his report for that year he talked about a "postage stamp printed on embossed paper." He said that in this process "the fibres of the paper being broken, cancelling marks almost necessarily penetrate, so that they cannot easily be removed without destroying the stamp." This process was covered by a patent owned by a Charles F. Steel of Brooklyn, New York, who apparently had never actually built a machine to emboss the stamps but sold his concept to the National Bank Note Company.

In this process, which became known as "grilling," the fibers of the paper were broken by grills to such an extent that the canceling ink would soak into the paper, so that washing or cleaning the stamp would be virtually impossible. The grills were applied to the sheets of stamps by means of a relatively simple machine which featured a roller with small, raised pyramids on it. When the sheet was rolled through the machine, tiny pyramid-like protuberances were produced on the sheet—an embossing process.

On Randall's instructions, these grilled stamps were first produced in the summer of 1867, beginning with the three-cent stamp, and over the next eighteen months other grilled stamps appeared. These have sometimes been called the issue of 1867, but that is not quite correct because those stamps were the same issue of 1861, but now produced with grills, and they might be more properly called the grilled stamps of 1867–69.

At first, the grill was designed to cover the entire face of the stamp, but problems with the grilled stamps, which had a tendency to tear anywhere except along the perforations, soon led to a reduction of the grilled area so

The first grilled stamps produced in 1867 had the grill impression covering the entire face of the stamp. A few of these "A" grills were produced before the contractor decided to reduce the size of the grilled area to a small block on each stamp. This cover, of August 1867, bears a single three-cent "A" grill canceled at Minneapolis. The cover is addressed to General Benjamin Harrison, later to be elected President of the United States. (National Philatelic Collection)

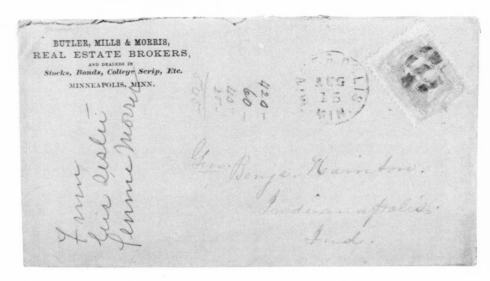

that it covered only a small part of each stamp. The many rollers used to produce the grilled stamps were machined without much regard for the size of the grill that would result, and thus we find grills in a variety of sizes, which were produced in varying quantities and which are very much in demand by today's philatelists.

One of the most desirable grill types is the "D" grill, an embossed area of twelve by fourteen millimeters. This October 2, 1868, cover from Savannah, Georgia, bears a very fine example of this elusive stamp. (National Philatelic Collection)

An even more important contribution by Alexander Randall was the issue of the first federal pictorial postage stamps. Prior to that issue, all federal postage stamps had featured a picture of some political figure, alive or dead, although, as we noted, some of the earlier postmasters' provisionals bore other designs, such as the one produced at the post office in St. Louis, and the carrier stamp of 1851, which featured an eagle. Now other types of designs were to be included in this new federal issue, which was planned and contracted by Randall in 1868. He wanted to release the stamps on February 1, 1869, but they were not ready until April of that year, when a new postmaster general of the new administration was already in office. Nevertheless, they are Randall's stamps, and that pictorial issue of 1869 is one of the most popular of all U.S. issues among today's stamp collectors.

In June 1868 Randall advertised for printing bids on a new issue, specifying stamps of a variety of both sizes and designs. He eventually awarded a four-year contract to the same National Bank Note Company at a price of 25½ cents per thousand stamps, "embossed like the stamps now in use." The Philadelphia firm of Butler & Carpenter immediately protested, claiming that it had submitted a lower bid, which in fact it had. A congressional committee was then appointed to investigate the matter, but found in favor of the bid award to National Bank Note basically because that firm now owned the patent for the embossing process which the bid offer specified.

The Post Office Department contract with National Bank Note was signed on December 12, 1868, and in it are the specifications for the first pictorial stamps. There were provisions for the usual "heads"—Franklin, Washington, and Lincoln—but there were new specifications for the first pictorials: a post-horse and rider, a locomotive, a steamship, the landing of Columbus, the Declaration of Independence, and an eagle and shield. All of these stamps were to be printed in two colors, and they were to be in denominations ranging from one cent to ninety cents.

The delivery of these new stamps could indeed have been made by February 1, 1869, except for the fact that when the design proposals—or "essays" as they are called in philately—were first submitted by National Bank

Note, they were rejected by Randall, including all the new pictorials listed in the contract, and an additional stamp depicting the surrender of General Burgoyne at Saratoga during the Revolutionary War.

Finally, the essays were approved, and the first stamps of the issue of 1869 began to appear in April of that year. The previous issue of 1861 was not demonetized and these stamps continued to be used as long as the supply lasted; in fact, some postmasters seemed in no hurry to stock the new stamps until they were out of the earlier issue. The new issue was not printed in great numbers, because, beautiful as the stamps were in design and production, they were not at all popular with the public, which considered the stamps to be "too busy" or "cluttered" in appearance. After some of the individual designs were ridiculed in the press, the issue was replaced with a more traditional set of portrait stamps within a year. The public's attitude toward this first pictorial issue might have been different if the most attractive designs had not been reserved for the high-value stamps, which were used almost exclusively for foreign mails and thus were not seen by the largest part of the public.

ひ

The stamps of the issue of 1869 were:

One cent. A head of Benjamin Franklin, after a bust by Houdon, looking to the left, surrounded by a circle of pearls. "U.S. POSTAGE" on a curved tablet at the top; "ONE CENT" in two similar tablets at the bottom, with the numeral "1" in a small panel between the words. Colors, buff, brown orange, dark brown orange.

Two cents. A true pictorial, this stamp features a post-horse and rider dashing off to the left, surrounded by ornamental scrollwork. Colors, brown, pale brown, dark brown, and yellow brown. The design drew sarcastic and unflattering comments from the beginning, such as the statement in the *New York Herald* that the picture "represents Booth's death ride into Maryland." Horsemen also criticized the position of the legs of the horse, since it appears to be leaping rather than galloping.

Three cents. Another pictorial, featuring a locomotive moving toward the right and surrounded by ornamental scrollwork. Colors, ultramarine, pale ultramarine, dark ultramarine, dark blue. The printer delivered 386,475,900 of these stamps—the most common in the 1869 issue.

Six cents. Head of Washington, after Stuart's painting, within a circular opening lined with pearls with a square frame, tesselated near the corners. Colors, ultramarine, pale ultramarine.

Ten cents. A pictorial featuring a shield on which is perched an eagle with outstretched wings. The whole design is surmounted by thirteen stars arranged in a semicircle. Colors, yellow, yellowish orange.

Twelve cents. Another pictorial, featuring an ocean steamship surrounded by ornamental scrollwork. The vessel was actually the *SS Adriatic*, which at the time of her completion was one of the great wooden paddle liners of the day. Brookman believes that this is the finest design of the 1869 series. Colors, green, deep green, bluish green, yellowish green.

Fifteen cents. Another pictorial, showing the landing of Columbus, after the painting by Vanderlyn in the Capitol in Washington, with ornamental

The 1869 pictorial issue. (R. Meyersburg collection)

scrollwork at top and bottom. Colors, red brown and blue, dark red brown and blue, pale red brown and blue. This stamp exists in two types—a minor change having been made to the frame around the central picture.

Twenty-four cents. A pictorial showing the signing of the Declaration of Independence, after the painting by Trumbull in the Capitol, with ornamental scrollwork at top and bottom. The engraving, by James Smillie, has been acclaimed as one of the finest examples of engraving of the time, since the features of the six principal figures in the picture are so clear and distinct.

Thirty cents. A pictorial featuring an eagle with outstretched wings perched on a shield with flags grouped at either side. What keeps this stamp from being truly handsome is the fact that the words "THIRTY CENTS" are rather artlessly superimposed across the bottom on the shield. Colors, blue and carmine, pale blue and carmine, blue and dark carmine.

Ninety cents. A portrait of Lincoln (from a photograph) in an oval, surrounded by ornamental scrollwork. Colors, carmine and black, carmine rose and black.

In addition to being the first pictorial issue, the 1869 stamps were also the first bicolored stamps produced in America. As might be expected, there were some problems—the second color having occasionally been printed upside-down on the sheet. These "inverted centers" were not made in any quantity, and today copies of the fifteen-, twenty-four, and thirty-cent stamps showing this early printing error are avidly sought by collectors.

404

General C. B. Norton.
8. Place de la Madeleine
Paris
France.

This cover, mailed at Cape Elizabeth Depot, Maine, was evidently meant to be prepaid to France as a double-weight letter under "direct" service. The payment for this service was made up with four two-cent stamps and four three-cent stamps, for a total of twenty cents. The direct service would only have paid the letter as far as the French border, however. When the letter reached New York, the foreign division clerk found that it was of a weight that allowed it to travel via British mail prepaid to destination. The cover was routed by British mail and sixteen cents were credited to Britain, two times the single-letter credit of eight cents. The continued confusion caused by the complicated foreign rate structure was to lend weight to the arguments of those farsighted postal administrators who, in the years ahead, would lay the groundwork for a simple and efficient international rate system. (National Philatelic Collection)

The issue of the first federal pictorials in 1869 marked the end of the first major era in the history of the United States postage stamp.

The postage stamp, of course, was to have a continuing and important history in the nation. In fact, John Creswell, the new postmaster general in 1869, would put out yet another new issue of stamps the following year, the Bank Note issue of 1870. Ideas proposed in the 1860s would find fruition in the 1870s. For instance, Montgomery Blair had sent representatives to the first International Postal Conference in Paris in 1863 and this first inconclusive attempt at international cooperation would finally be accomplished in the Universal Postal Union of 1874. There would also be new and lower rates, new issues of stamps, and new services such as special delivery and rural free delivery.

But by 1869 the American stamp had come through its first major cycle, beginning back in 1842 with that first stamp, issued privately by the City Despatch Post, and then through those years of tentative progress which saw the nation inching toward the development of the full type of postal system that was then functioning in England. In 1847 the first federal stamp was issued, and then there were the new lower rates and new stamp issues; finally, the stamp was made compulsory in 1856.

That period also saw significant developments in both the stamp itself and the way it was used, such as the perforated issue and registered mail and money orders. The stamp also became transcontinental as new and quicker mail routes were opened to the West. And the stamp was, in a sense, bifurcated during those cruel days of the Civil War when there were two sets of stamps and two postal systems in America. Finally, with the Union

A single three-cent stamp of the 1869 issue was added to this three-cent stamped envelope to cover the double postage required on this cover from Indianapolis, Indiana, to Louisville, Kentucky. Both the stamp and the envelope were canceled with a fancy carved-leaf design handstamp. (National Philatelic Collection)

preserved, the postal system was unified during the difficult time of the Reconstruction, and the final stamps of the period were issued: first, the grilled stamps and then the pictorials. Those twenty-seven years, from 1842 to 1869, represent a period of immense and significant progress in postal matters, a period in which the United States postage stamp was born and came to maturity.

There was now, truly, an American issue.

Appendix: The Distribution of the First Federal Stamps in 1847

THE FIRST AMERICAN FEDERAL ISSUE OF STAMPS—A FIVE-CENT Benjamin Franklin and a ten-cent George Washington—became valid on July 1, 1847, and was to remain valid for four years. These stamps were not compulsory, and, as we noted in the text, their use was modest during the entire term of the issue until 1851, when they were demonetized in favor of the new issue. The following figures show which post offices in the nation received these new postage stamps from Washington, D.C., during the first year of the issue. The time period covered here is for the government fiscal year—that is, July 1, 1847, to June 30, 1848.

Town	Total 5c	Total 10c
ALABAMA		
Mobile	4,200	3,900
Huntsville	1,200	400
Montgomery	1,200	700
Tuscumbia	200	100
CONNECTICUT		
New London	1,200	200
New Haven	7,300	1,100
Hartford	6,600	700
Bridgeport	800	200
DELAWARE		
Wilmington	3,400	300
DISTRICT OF COLUMBIA	10,380	3,100
FLORIDA		
Tallahassee	600	400
Apalachicola	700	900
Quincy	600	200
GEORGIA		
Macon	3,000	1,500
Savannah	1,200	400
Milledgeville	1,200	400
Augusta	1,200	400
Madison	400	100
ILLINOIS		
Chicago	1,200	400
Quincy	1,000	500
Springfield	400	400
Jacksonville	400	200

Town	Total 5c	Total 10c
INDIANA		
Indianapolis	1,200	400
Lafayette	500	400
Madison	1,400	600
Evansville	1,400	600
Fort Wayne	600	200
New Albany	400	200
KENTUCKY		
Louisville	7,400	4,300
Maysville	1,600	600
Lexington	1,800	600
Hickman	200	200
Paris	400	100
LOUISIANA		
New Orleans	9,000	6,000
Baton Rouge	400	200
MAINE		
Augusta	1,200	400
Bangor	2,200	400
Portland	4,800	600
Eastport	1,900	1,200
Calais	1,000	300
MARYLAND		
Baltimore	27,500	9,300
Cumberland	2,500	300
Annapolis	1,000	200

Town	Total 5c	Total 10c
MASSACHUSETTS		
Boston	80,000	10,000
Worcester	3,200	400
Springfield	4,200	400
Charlestown	400	100
Roxbury	600	100
Greenfield	1,200	100
Newburyport	400	—
Great Barrington	700	200
New Bedford	800	—
Northampton	1,000	—
Plymouth	400	100
MICHIGAN		
Detroit	2,000	1,000
Monroe	300	100
MISSISSIPPI		
Jackson	400	300
MISSOURI		
St. Louis	8,400	6,300
NEW JERSEY		
Newark	600	200
Jersey City	600	200
NEW HAMPSHIRE		
Concord	1,200	400
Dover	500	200
Exeter	400	100

Town	Total 5c	Total 10c
NEW YORK		
New York	190,000	55,000
Buffalo	10,600	4,200
Syracuse	3,200	400
Geneva	2,200	400
Albany	13,400	800
Utica	15,400	800
Batavia	4,200	1,500
Rochester	10,500	3,500
Troy	8,400	400
Palmyra	600	200
Owego	600	200
Oswego	600	200
Lockport	4,400	2,300
Penn Yan	600	200
Saugerties	200	100
Lewiston	300	100
Binghamton	1,900	100
West Point	600	200
Attica	2,000	1,000
Sacket's Harbor	600	200
Newark	200	100
Dansville	400	100
Bath	400	100
Elmira	200	100
Keeseville	400	100
NORTH CAROLINA		
Raleigh	1,200	400
Elizabeth City	300	100

Town	Total 5c	Total 10c
OHIO		
Cincinnati	14,000	9,000
Cleveland	7,800	3,100
Columbia	4,800	1,600
Toledo	1,600	1,200
Steubenville	600	200
Norwalk	600	200
Canton	200	100
Dayton	1,000	400
Warren	300	100
Marietta	800	300
Cuyahoga Falls	1,000	300
Zanesville	400	200
Newark	400	100
PENNSYLVANIA		
Philadelphia	88,000	22,000
Pottsville	2,600	300
Erie	600	400
Pittsburgh	2,800	800
Washington	600	200
Uniontown	200	100
Meadville	400	100
Lewiston	400	—
RHODE ISLAND		
Providence	7,200	900
Pawtucket	1,200	400
Westerly	400	100
SOUTH CAROLINA		
Charleston	8,200	4,400
Georgetown	1,200	400
Camden	1,800	600

Town	Total 5c	Total 10c
TENNESSEE		
Nashville	2,200	900
Jackson	200	100
TEXAS		
Galveston	600	400
Houston	200	200
VERMONT		
Middlebury	10,300	600
Montpelier	3,600	200
Bennington	500	100
VIRGINIA		
Richmond	5,800	3,100
Norfolk	1,200	900
Wheeling	1,200	400
Kanawha C. H.	600	200
Theological Seminary	200	100
University of Va.	400	200
Fredericksburg	200	—
Martinsburg	200	100
WISCONSIN		
Milwaukee	600	200
Racine	400	200

(Note: the above *delivered* postage stamps of 1847–48 do not, of course, necessarily represent all the stamps actually *sold* during that first year of the federal issue. As we noted in the text, it is difficult to estimate exactly how many of those first U.S. stamps were actually used.)

Select Bibliography

ALEXANDER, THOMAS J. *Simpson's U.S. Postal Markings 1851–1861.* 2d ed., rev. Columbus, Ohio: U.S. Philatelic Classics Society, 1979.

A comprehensive updating of Tracy W. Simpson's 1959 work (see below). This is a valuable reference for the postal historian.

ASHBROOK, STANLEY B. *The United States One Cent Stamp of 1851–1857.* 2 vols. New York: H.L. Linquist, 1938.

One of the great classics of philatelic literature, this work contains everything the reader could possibly want to know about the production and use of one denomination of one issue of stamps. An updated version of volume 1 has been produced by Mortimer L. Neinken (see below).

ASHBROOK, STANLEY B. *Notes on 19th Century U.S. Postal History* (commonly known as "Special Services"). 1951–1957.

This very useful work was published serially by the author and circulated only to a small group of dedicated philatelic scholars. It contains detailed information on rates and usages of United States stamps. Generally this set is available only through specialized philatelic libraries.

BROOKMAN, LESTER G. *The United States Postage Stamps of the 19th Century.* 3 vols. New York: H.L. Lindquist, 1966.

An outstanding and exhaustive work covering the development and use of each issue of stamps. While these volumes do not contain the depth of information represented in "single issue" studies, such as the Ashbrook book mentioned above, the treatment of each issue is more than adequate for all but the most advanced student, and the scope of this work is unparalleled in recent years.

CHASE, CARROLL. *The 3¢ Stamp of the United States 1851–1857 Issue.* Hammondsport, N.Y.: J.O. Moore, 1929.

Another outstanding reference of the "single issue" type. There is some outdated information contained in the sections dealing with the use of these stamps, but the overall work is indispensable. All of the major catalog listings for this issue are based on Chase's work.

DIETZ, AUGUST. *The Postal Service of the Confederate States of America.* Richmond, Va.: Press of the Dietz Printing Co., 1929.

The pioneer work on Confederate postal history. While some of the information is now outdated, this work has remained preeminent in its subject area for over fifty years.

DIETZ, AUGUST, ET AL. *Dietz Confederate States Catalog and Handbook*. Richmond, Va.: The Dietz Press, 1959.

The latest and most complete guide to the stamps and envelopes of the Confederate States of America. This classic work will soon be replaced by an updated version.

HAHN, MANNEL. *Postal Markings of the United States 1847–1851*. Chicago: William R. Stewart, 1938.

A guide to the distribution and use of the five- and ten-cent stamps of the 1847 issue. While the information on markings is far from complete, the charts showing the quantities of the 1847 stamps which were distributed to each of the post offices are quite valuable to the student of this first postal-adhesive issue.

HARGEST, GEORGE E. *History of Letter Post Communication between the United States and Europe 1845–1875*. Washington, D.C.: Smithsonian Institution Press, 1971.

The first and finest guide to transatlantic mail services, and the postal treaties and conventions that set the rates.

LUFF, JOHN N. *The Postage Stamps of the United States* New York: The Scott Stamp and Coin Co., 1902.

As the first major comprehensive work on United States stamps, this book was for years considered the "bible" of serious collectors. It is now known that Luff included a great deal of undocumentable or just plain incorrect information in this classic. Very entertaining reading.

NEINKEN, MORTIMER L. *The United States One Cent Stamp of 1851–1861*. Columbus, Ohio: U.S. Philatelic Classics Society, 1972.

A superb updating of the classic work by Stanley B. Ashbrook (see above) and covering the same subject matter as in volume 1 of the earlier work.

REMELE, CHARLES W. *United States Railroad Postmarks 1837–1861*. State College, Pa.: U.S. 1851–60 Unit, No. 11, of the American Philatelic Society, 1958.

A seminal work, now outdated, listing the markings and outlining the histories of the various railroads of this period.

RICH, WESLEY E. *The History of the United States Post Office to the Year 1829*. Cambridge, Mass.: Harvard University Press, 1924.

A classic work which clearly chronicles the development of mail services in North America, first under colonial rule and later as the United States. Highly technical in parts, this is an essential reference for the serious student.

SCHEELE, CARL H. *A Short History of the Mail Service*. Washington, D.C.: Smithsonian Institution Press, 1970.

An accurate, uncomplicated, and well written history of United States postal services from the colonial period. Also a brief survey of the ancient antecedents of our modern postal systems.

SIMPSON, TRACY W. *United States Postal Markings and Related Mail Services, 1851–1861*. Berkeley, Calif.: T.W. Simpson, 1959.

This was the first attempt at a scholarly and comprehensive guide to the postal markings and services of this period. This outdated classic has now been enlarged and revised (see Alexander above).

SMITH, A. D. *The Develpment of Rates of Postage*. London: George Allen & Unwin, 1917.

A well-written and most informative study of the development of postal services in the United States and Europe.

TOWLE, C.L., AND MEYER, H.A. *Railroad Postmarks of the United States 1861–1866*. Columbus, Ohio: U.S. Philatelic Classics Society, 1968.

An outstanding guide to the rail routes and railroad postal markings used during the golden age of the iron horse.

TOWLE, CHARLES L. *The United States Transit Markings Catalog 1837 to 1974. Volume 1, 1837–1886*. Mobile Post Office Society, 1975.

A skillful updating of both the Remele and Towle/ Meyer (see above) handbooks on railroad postal marks.

A Note on Philatelic Periodicals

Much of the outstanding philatelic research work of the last eighty years has been published as articles in the many serial publications this field has supported. Some of the journals which regularly include articles on United States postage stamps and postal history are listed below:

The American Philatelist
The Chronicle of the U.S. Classic Postal Issues
The Collectors Club Philatelist
The Confederate Philatelist
The Congress Book
Linn's Stamp News
The S.P.A. Journal

Acknowledgments

WE WANT TO THANK THE MANY PEOPLE WHO ASSISTED US IN THE preparation of this volume. Among them was Robert Meyersburg, who so generously allowed us to use many items in his remarkable philatelic collection and also gave us access to his research files. Furthermore, both he and Gordon Torrey kindly reviewed the manuscript for us before publication. Special thanks are due to Sheila Sheehan, who typed the manuscript, and very special thanks to Edward F. Rivinus, senior science editor at the Smithsonian Institution Press, who encouraged and assisted us from the very beginning of this project.

Index

(Italicized numbers indicate that the reference is in the caption on that page.)